252.06

Heart to Heart

Heart to Heart

messages that warm the heart
and exalt the Savior

Robert G. Lee

Broadman Press/Nashville, Tennessee

Contents

Heart to Heart

1.
Roses Will
Bloom Again

My text is from Isaiah 35:1. "The desert shall rejoice, and blossom as the rose."

When we go back and see what people have written about the rose and roses, we find a great many wonderful things.

Emerson said, "The sea opulent, plentiful and strong, as beautiful as a rose on a June day."

And Mrs. Browning, the woman Shakespeare of England, wrote: "Roses aplenty, roses aplenty, and nightingale, one for every twenty, and when you put it in a drawer and try to give it a name, all these things just bring it to shame."

Showing us the inadequacy of words really to describe the rose.

Another poet said: "The finest, the frailest kind of rose is more beautiful than the most skillful production of the rose by the sculptor's chisel."

And Keats said: "When they bring roses to me, when you brought roses to me, they had voices that whispered of peace and truth and love."

And another great poet said: "The rosebuds that put

their crimson lips together."

Another poet said:

"The wayside rose holds out its fragrant arms,

"And with its beauty our eye it charms."

Then, of course, we remember what Robert Burns said in his sweet Scotch language. He said:

"I pluck the rose when Phoebus comes in view,

"And to pluck it is like a kiss from her bonny mou."

("Mou," which means, of course, mouth.)

We could say many things that the poets have said about the rose. But we know that when we come to think of the beauty of the rose, that it puts the poet's pen· to test adequately to describe it, and it puts the orator's eloquence to a test to see if it can really see and say what the rose merits.

We remember, too, that the sculptor, who sometimes brings children unto God, raises children unto God from the sterile womb of stone, has spent hours trying to carve from marble the beauty of the rose.

We remember when we've come to think of the symmetry, fragrance, and softness of the rose amid the thorns, that the painter's brush sometimes is held in a hand that hesitates because of its woeful inadequacy fully to portray all the rose is and has ever been in the thoughts and minds of men.

Sometimes we see the roses adorning the little cottage in the pines, and sometimes adding beauty to the king's palace, and sometimes the rose is put upon beauteous brow, and so many times we have seen the rose at the wedding altar, and many times we have seen roses placed upon the tomb.

When we come to think of all that philosophers have said in their meditations about the rose, and all that singers have sung about the rose—like "My Wild Irish Rose" and "Moonlight and Roses" which always delight my heart and bless my life—we come to understand something, just a little bit of something of what Isaiah meant when he said: "The desert . . . shall blossom as a rose." The desert, the desolate desert, without any vegetation in it; the desolate desert, the drear desert, with the cracks in the ground that seem like parched lips that cry for rain; the desert, desolate without a flower or fountain in all of its weary miles; the desert, with its hot sands that burn the eyes as the wind blows across them; the hot desert, the desolate desert, the dreary desert, the desert without pools of water, the desert without flowers, the desert with the jackals that howl and the wolves that prowl, and the serpents that crawl.

The desolate, dead desert, without any flowers or fountains in all its vast areas.

And Isaiah said: "That desert shall rejoice, and blossom as a rose."

Where the hiss of the serpent was heard, and where the howl of the wolf disturbed the stillness of the night, and where the coughing of the coyotes was unpleasant to hear, and where you could find nothing but dust when you wanted water, and nothing but some kind of gravel bareness when you wanted food, that desolate desert, said Isaiah the prophet, shall blossom, shall rejoice, and blossom as the rose.

That's a wonderful thing that Isaiah said. But what sort of person was Isaiah? Among the constellation of the prophets, Isaiah was very mighty and very beautiful. His smallest whisper was as loud to the ears of the people as a thunderclap in the time of storm. His sweetest words were like breezes laden with honeysuckle fragrance. In his preaching always were the thunders and the lightnings of Sinai and the foregleams of Calvary and the growl of the Assyrian wolf, God's instrument of judgment against his people who had failed to love him and failed to serve him and who had forsaken him.

God came to the place where he said: I'm bored with your sacrifices and your empty worship times. I'm tired and sick of you because you have forsaken me and have gone out after the idolatries of the day.

We find how Isaiah fought very strongly against these kings who had led the people away from God into the idolatries of his day. They wouldn't listen to him. They even laughed at him.

Then Isaiah, somewhat in despair but guided by the Holy Spirit, telling them about the Assyrian nation that would come and take them into captivity, showed how one day, even though that should be, a remnant should behave, should be saved, and God who demanded holiness should, with this remnant, build a new house of holiness and truth upon the dead ashes of their wrecked life, as it was as a desert.

So we come to find that he talked about how roses should bloom again. There had come to that nation the wintertime, and the religious life of the people had been like trees frozen by the breeze and stripped of their foliage by the terrible blizzardy winds.

As he thought of that, he thought of how the streams, the voices of the streams, frozen beneath the ice, had nothing to say to bird or beast or man, and how spring and summertime were asleep beneath the heavy blankets of snow, and how the desolate desert of national life should someday blossom; he spoke very hopefully about the time when the roses should bloom again, when he said that

God would put in the wilderness the fir and the cedar and the oil tree and the pine and he would also put the box tree together and they shall rejoice together (Isa. 41:19).

Then he said that God would comfort Zion. God would comfort her waste places. God would make the wilderness to be as Eden. He would make the desert to be as the garden of the Lord, and in the desert there would be joy and thanksgiving and rejoicing.

Oh, what a dread, desolate picture on the one side and the very beautiful picture on the other side! The desert and then the garden of the Lord. The wilderness and then Eden. The voice of despair and the voice of rejoicing. The voice of ingratitude and the voice of thanksgiving. He said that day will come through the remnant that God shall bring back from captivity after the Assyrian scourge has finished with you, and he shall build his house of holiness and truth upon the desolate desert places and it shall rejoice and blossom as the rose.

Let's see how that has been true in so many instances.

It was true in Noah's day when, after the terrible time when God hurled oceans over mountain ranges and drowned a world that had hated him where they should have loved him and should have obeyed him, where they had forsaken him and defied him, the roses bloomed again.

I think of Abraham, when God told him to take his century plant, his century flower, his only son, Isaac, whom he loved, and offer him there on the mountaintop.

When Abraham did what God said, making the three days' journey, he came in sight of the mountain, and he said to his servant: "Abide ye here with the ass; and I and the lad go yonder and worship" (Gen. 22:5).

That was a night, an hour of despair, an hour of night, an hour of hopelessness, an hour when they should worship God but one half of the congregation would kill the other half.

Oh! That was a desert in so many ways to Abraham. But when Abraham had the knife ready to take Isaac's life, God called Abraham's name and after Abraham answered God told him not to kill Isaac.

And then Abraham turned and saw a ram with his horns caught in the thicket, and he took that and offered it instead of Isaac.

In other words, the desert became an Eden, a garden of the Lord, and where there had been nothing but desolation, there now the roses were blooming again.

I think of David, pursued by King Saul.

David, an outlaw, running from King Saul as a hare would run from the hound, and as a mouse would seek to hide itself from the eagle's talons, and as the lamb sought refuge from the wolf, and David said: "I shall now perish one day by the hand of Saul."

That was a desert for David, but there came a time when the roses bloomed for David, and they bloomed around a throne, and they bloomed clustering around a scepter and a crown when they crowned him King of Judah, and then a little bit later, King of Israel and Judah.

The roses bloomed again!

Then I think of Joseph's being sold into slavery into Egypt, and put in jail because of the lying of Potiphar's wife.

I think of Jacob, who had seen the coat that his sons had brought to him, stained with an animal's blood, and he said: "It is my son's coat; an evil beast has devoured him."

And for twenty years Jacob had been in the desert because of the loss of Joseph whom he loved very much.

But when his sons in the time of the famine went down to Egypt and found that Joseph was the governor of the land and wearing the keys of the kingdom at his girdle, then Jacob found that his desert had been made an Eden; his desert had been made the garden of the Lord; and in his desert there was thanksgiving and the voice of joy and rejoicing and prayer.

Yes, these men went back after they found out that Joseph was the governor, and he had made himself known to them, and they went back to Jacob, who for twenty years had had a desert without any roses to bloom in it. They said: "Joseph is yet alive, and he is governor over all the land of Egypt."

And Jacob's heart fainted within him at the news, but when he saw the wagons loaded with the corn that they had brought back from the land of plenty to the land of famine, he said: "I will go and see him."

And, so Jacob, in one of the most beautiful stories in all the Bible to me, old Jacob made that journey and saw his boy whom he hadn't seen for twenty years, and saw him as governor and saw him as a man of power.

In the desert, Jacob found that God changed it to an Eden, to a garden of the Lord, and there was the voice of thanksgiving and rejoicing.

And I think of those four hundred years that are set forth after the prophecy of Malachi before we have any Gospel of Matthew. *Four hundred years* it was a desert time, a time of desolation, a time when the wilderness and not the flower garden prevailed!

And then came a man clothed in camel's hair!

And then came a man descending upon the iniquities of his day with a torch in one hand and a sword in the other!

There came a day when this wilderness preacher came, interpreting the voice of betrothal as a friend of the Bridegroom, pointing out Jesus as the Lamb of God!

Then came Jesus at a time when religion and idolatry were holding hands and when the hands of hypocrisy were playing upon the harp of formalism and ritualism and icy nothingness!

Oh, what a time it was!

Then came some shepherds and worshiped at a manger above which heaven had put out a bright star.

And at that time, at that very time, old Athens, the intellectual center of the world, was drunk with the wine of skepticism, and old Rome was asleep yonder by the river, asleep under the music of a tyrant's voice and the Roman Colosseum tied the cruelty of the Roman Empire and when the Roman fist was upon the purse of the Jewish nation and the Roman heel upon its chest. At that same time, old Persia was wearing on her brow a funeral wreath, and old Egypt was asleep with her head in the lap of the sphinx, Egypt, where God had wrought his marvelous miracles through the plagues, and yet they had not believed so very much in God at all amidst all their gods.

Then came some shepherds to worship at a cattle trough in a barn.

Then came some Wise Men with their gifts of gold and frankincense and myrrh.

And for this world, so long a desolate waste, the roses bloomed through him who was called the Rose of Sharon, the Lily of the valley, the fairest of ten thousand, the One altogether lovely.

Then you remember how this Rose of Sharon was put under the terrible heel of death yonder on the cross, how Jesus died. And the day when Jesus died, nobody called him Lord except a dying thief, and the kingdom about which he had talked, in the minds of the disciples, had shrunk to the narrow dimensions of a grave. Death, with his skeleton heel, had crushed out the life of the Lily of the valley and the Rose of Sharon fair; death, whose only pleasure is fountains of falling tears, had closed the eyes that shed tears over Jerusalem. Death, whose only music is the sob of broken hearts, had hushed the mouth that spake as never man spake.

And the disciples saw all their hopes go down beyond that bloody hill where the crosses were and where the earthquake rolled forth its dirge, and where darkness came down at midday and midnight said to noonday, "Get off the throne of the universe and let me sit there." And noonday did midnight's bidding.

The roses were all dead, it seemed.

The Rose of Sharon seemed to be dead forever and would never bloom.

But on that third day morning, up from the grave he arose!

The roses bloomed again, and the desert was as Eden, and the desolate place was as the garden of the Lord, and the disciples had their voice of thanksgiving and rejoicing when they said to Thomas: "We have seen the Lord," and they were glad that they saw him.

Now, can we make this a very practical thing to apply to your own heart and life?

Is your life a desert place?

Is your life a wilderness?

Do you want it to be an Eden?

Do you want it to be the garden of the Lord?

Well, it can be if you will only let the Master have his way with you.

Is it an ill-health blizzard that has taken the roses out of your life's garden?

Well, God cares because God knows.

And he knows our downsitting and our uprising, and he is acquainted with all of our ways.

Is it a loneliness desert where you seem not to have companionship?

Remember what a friend you can have in Jesus.

Is it a misunderstanding, desolate desert. Desert, desert. Desert of desolation, desolation, desolation, where the roses of kindness have died?

Is it a desolate desert of abuse, where joy has breathed its last and no roses bloom? There are just thorns for you and maybe some of the devil's poison ivy?

Well, remember this: Jesus is alive, and Jesus cares.

If your family circle broken? Has it been broken and you wonder about some things?

Has bereavement come and torn some tender flowers you loved so much from your garden? Have you followed the hearse? Have you stood by the grave? Have you heard people sob?

Well, maybe it's a kind of a blizzard like that that has left you in the wintertime.

Perhaps you are not today as great a Christian as God wanted you to be, and somehow you have let the winter blizzards of skepticism, doubt, infidelity, and worldliness blight all the flowers in your life's garden.

Well, where are you going to find any help for a time like that?

Hear these words of Isaiah: "Come now, and let us reason together, saith the Lord: though your sins be as scarlet, they shall be as white as snow; though they be red like crimson, they shall be as wool" (1:18).

What did He do that that should be?
He bore our sins in His own Body on the Tree.

Has sin gotten the best of you? Has something crept
into your life, gnawing at it and blighting it like a frost?
Is something corroding your life like rust, and dulling the
edge of your spiritual weapons?

If your life a kind of a desert swept by the blizzard
where no flowers bloom?

Well, there is One to whom you can go.

And remember that the rags will be changed into riches,
and the pewter will be changed to gold, and if you've
lain among the pots and have become blackened and
smutty, smut-covered, as Isaiah, the prophet, spoke about
it: "You shall be as a dog whose wings are silver."

That's what God says, talking about the time when the
roses shall bloom again.

Jesus came to this earth, and He knew what it was to
have roses for awhile.

Robert Browning pictured that in his wonderful poem
called, "The Patriot." The poet said that that day they
gave him a great parade, just like they gave Jesus a triumphal entry. He said:

> "Was roses, roses all the way
> And myrtle mixed in my path
> Like man, mad, and all the
> Housetops were gay. I could
> Have asked for the Sun yonder
> in the sky and the people would
> have said, 'You could have it.' "

But another day the patriot rode down the street and
he said:

"I feel the blood flowing down my face from the bricks they throw at me."

It was like that with Jesus. He came with the galleries of heaven giving him applause.

He came with the sweetest, purest of a woman to be his mother.

He came, with a man who has never had the praise he should have had, with Joseph to take care of Mary.

He came with the tender ministrations of her love.

He came when the Wise Men worshiped him and the shepherds worshiped him.

Those were rose days for Jesus.

But there came the day when Herod wanted to kill him, and in order to try to kill him, killed all the boy babies under two years of age.

And then it was that later on the Sanhedrin was deployed against him.

The army of Rome was against him.

Forces, evil forces from the palaces of the Caesars were against him, and these ragged folks of the mob of the streets joined in with the gentlemen of the palace to cry: "Away with him! Kill him! Kill him!"

One day they picked up stones to stone him to death, and Jesus said: "For which of my works do you stone me? Would you stone me because I made the blind to see and the deaf to hear and the fevers to leave bodies that wracked with pain?

"Would you stone me because I cleanse lepers and make crazy men have their minds restored? Would you stone me because I went into sick rooms and healed the sick and in the cemeteries and raised the dead? For which of my works would you stone me?"

But in their hearts they stoned him long before they

crucified him.

Great forces rode out from hell against him. Then against these assaulting forces Jesus lifted up his own banner of love; and who gathered at this banner of love? A few shoremen, fishermen gathered. A woman with a broken alabaster box gathered under his banner, and a widow with two mites gathered under his banner. And a rich publican called Zacchaeus gathered under his banner. And a few men, positionless and moneyless and with no political power, gathered.

And it is no wonder, it is no wonder that people asked him why he didn't surrender to these forces.

But he wouldn't take a step backward. He said: "I have come to seek and to save the lost. I have come to bring people out of their bondage and sorrow and night into my freedom, gladness, and light. I have come to cut the shackles off the wrists of people.

"I will not take a step back. I will not refuse to go to the cross. I will tread out the last grape of the last cluster. I will take the last step of the last mile. Though every step be punctured with pain, I will take it because I came to seek and to save that which was lost."

Oh, it seemed that these were all thorns. It seemed they were all thorns for Jesus. And he had his enemies who watched in the house into which he went and when he came out.

They watched him when he ate and with whom he ate.

They watched him when he drank and what he drank.

They listened to what he said and then found fault with what he said.

And he who went about doing good was followed by the hounds of hell in the person of his enemies until Jesus had to say one day to his disciples: "If the world hates you, just remember, it hated me before it hated you."

Oh, there were thorns amid all the roses that Jesus ever had upon this earth.

And, oh, I couldn't begin to tell you how I feel toward that woman who came and washed his feet with her tears and wiped them with the hairs of her head.

Oh, what roses were they amid the thorns that Jesus had to pierce him nearly every step of the way. "He was wounded for our transgressions, he was bruised for our iniquities" (Isa. 53:5).

I remember reading years ago about how Lady Kincaid talked about the Prince of Wales, who later became King George. One day after the First World War they took the king to visit the hospital. They said: "There are thirty-six men more wounded and maimed than anybody else, and we would like for you, if you will, to see these men." And the Prince of Wales said: "Gladly will I."

And so the doctor guided him into one place and there were thirty men, all maimed and wounded, and he shook hands with some of them and spoke to many of them and was sympathetic with all of them.

He said: "But you told me there were thirty-six. I see only thirty."

They said: "Well, there were six others more maimed than are these, and we keep them in a ward to themselves, because it's best so to do."

The king said: "Well, let me see these six." And he went into this ward where the six men were, and he saw them, more maimed than the others, and he spoke to everyone of them kindly, and then he said: "But you said there were six here. Where's the other man."

They said: "Well, the other man was so maimed and marred we didn't want anybody to see him."

The king, the prince, who later became king, said: "Let me see him."

And they took him into a room where was one man by himself, blind and deaf, armless, legless.

When the prince of the nation saw him, he was stilled in his tracks. He looked at him, this blind and deaf man without any legs, without any arms, and he went over and stooped down and kissed him.

He said, as he kissed him: "Wounded for me. Wounded for me."

Oh, I think of how the Bible tells us how mercy and truth have met together and kissed.

I think of how this Book says: "Kiss the Son, lest he be angry with thee."

And, so, we can think of Jesus, who walked amid the thorns as the Rose of God.

We can look at him and say: "He was wounded for me. Those thorn punctures in his brow, that terrible hole in his side, where the savage spear drank its precious libation of his blood. It was for me he died. For me he was bruised for my transgressions and with his stripes I shall find healing."

Oh, so many times we think that the roses will never bloom again.

Sometimes in the storm, when the storm is on, and the thunder crashes, the sky is inky black, danger and fear and death, it seems, ride the clouds. Not a bird to be seen or heard, only that thunder and lightning.

But, when the morning dawned, the earth was wonderful. Its air was fresh and washed, and the grass and leaves and flowers were clean and greener than ever, since God washed the world.

The roses bloomed again.

And sometimes we thought when we heard the tramp of the soldiers and saw them go away into the night, and the whole divisions of trained men slipping away, while women wept and while mothers wept and children, the nation stricken with the necessity of armed conflict! How far away seemed the days of peace.

How far away roses seemed when Pearl Harbor came on us that December day. Yes, how terrible it was and how uncertain the future.

But peace did come and roses bloomed again, and somehow, since I know that we will never hear of God's death, and, somehow, since I believe we will never have any newspaper heralding the funeral of Christ Jesus, this world now that's hanging on an abyss, on a thread above an abyss, a world of desolation and Communism and hatred taught us of many people in the nations of the world, people today, fighting, killing each other, somehow, I believe that the roses will bloom again!

And then you remember that day when you thought you could never laugh again? That afternoon late in the day when you turned away from the cemetery alone, you left a loved one behind, and all black and shadowed as you went back, brokenhearted, to the vacant house where kind neighbors came in, preparing the lonely supper?

But, life crowded in the next morning with its cares and duties, very fortunate for all, and, lo, after awhile the roses bloomed again!

The disciples thought the roses would never bloom again when they knew that Jesus was in the grave.

But the roses did bloom!

And after the stress, after the stress and storm, the roses bloomed.

And after the storm, the sun shone.

And after the night, the dawn.

And after the trial, the glory after the struggle, and the victory!

Always the roses! Always, always, after seeming defeat and disaster, victory!

The roses bloom again!

And sometimes I think I would like to get my people to see what the old guide said to a tourist in the Alps mountains. They went to sleep. They slept pretty well that night, covered with their blankets. In the morning about four or five o'clock a great thunderstorm came. The lightning burned its zigzag paths and tearing to shreds the vestments, the black vestments of the storm clouds. The thunder boomed and the rocky mountains trembled under it.

And a tourist awoke the guide, and said: "Are we safe? It's terrible, this storm!"

And the old guide lifted up his face and said: "Friend, this is the way the morning dawns a lot of times in this land."

Oh, sometimes it's the way the morning dawns, these storms.

Sometimes it's the planting and blooming of the roses after the desert God's dealing with us!

And so if you are in the desert of unbelief and you are not saved, let Jesus have his way with you, and the roses of salvation will bloom in your life if in him you trust with repentance toward God and faith in the Lord Jesus Christ.

And so this is the invitation to any who have never trusted Christ. Trust in him, and the roses of salvation will fill your garden, and the roses of redemption will bloom in your desert place! Yes, they will!

2.
Seven Eyes on
One Stone

"Upon one stone shall be seven eyes" (Zech. 3:9). *There are two persons prominent in this text.* The first person is Zechariah, priest and prophet whose name means "one whom Jehovah remembers" and who is sometimes called "the Columbus of prophecy." He began his prophetic functions in the second year of Darius' reign, 520 years before Christ came from heaven's height to Bethlehem's barn. Zechariah's style—at one time conversational, at another poetical—varies with the subject. Usually, though Chaldeeisms occur occasionally, though the symbols he uses are frequently enigmatic, necessitating accompanying explanations, though graphic vividness is his unique merit, though he often introduces spiritual beings into his prophetic scenes, his messages are strongly hopeful, beautifully messianic, peacefully triumphant.

The second person brought before us in this text is Jesus. In the words of our text, Zechariah had none other in mind, for often, in the Bible, Jesus is called a stone—the Rock—and seldom without some attribute of distinction. In the seventeenth chapter of Exodus, he is presented as the smitten Rock. Four times in the thirty-second chapter

of Deuteronomy is he called the Rock. "He is the Rock,
his work is perfect"; "Jeshurun . . . lightly esteemed the
Rock of his salvation"; "Of the Rock that begat thee thou
art unmindful"; "For their rock is not as our Rock."

Note these words: "Neither is there any rock like our
God" (1 Sam. 2:2); "The Lord is my rock" (Ps. 18:2).
"Exalted be the God of the rock of my salvation"
(2 Sam. 22:47). "He only is my rock . . . the rock of my
strength, and my refuge" (Ps. 62:6-7); "And a man shall
be as an hiding place from the wind, and a covert from
the tempest; as rivers of water in a dry place, as the shadow
of a great rock in a weary land" (Isa. 32:2).

As the rock was smitten by Moses at Horeb, so was
Christ smitten—at Calvary. "We did esteem him stricken,
smitten of God" (Isa. 53:4). "Smite the shepherd, and the
sheep shall be scattered" (Zech. 13:7). There was no water
until the rock was smitten. "Behold, he smote the rock,
that the waters gushed out" (Ps. 78:20). This is true also
of Christ the Rock.

> "Let the water and the blood,
> From Thy wounded side which flowed,
> Be of sin the double cure,
> Save from wrath and make us pure."
>
> —Augustus M. Toplady

Peter calls Jesus "a living stone."

"Two whom coming, as unto a living stone, disallowed indeed of men, but chosen of God, and precious, ye also, as lively stones, are built up a spiritual
house, an holy priesthood, to offer up spiritual sacrifices, acceptable to God by Jesus Christ. Wherefore
also it is contained in the scripture, Behold I lay in

Zion a chief corner stone, elect, precious: and he that
believeth on him shall not be confounded. Unto you
therefore which believe he is precious: but unto them
which be disobedient, the stone which the builders
disallowed, the same is made the head of the corner"
(1 Pet. 2:4-7).

The Scriptures tell of four things taken from the rock.
All four are typical. Water came from the rock. "And that
Rock was Christ"—the Water of life. Fire came from the
rock. "Then the angel of the Lord put forth the end of
the staff that was in his hand, and touched the flesh and
the unleavened cakes; and there rose up fire out of the
rock, and consumed the flesh and the unleavened cakes"
(Judg. 6:21). And so "our God is a consuming fire"
(Heb. 12:29). Honey came from the rock. "With honey
out of the rock should I have satisfied thee" (Ps. 81:16).
The sweetest name on mortal tongue is Jesus. Oil came
from the rock. "He made him to suck . . . oil out of the
flinty rock" (Deut. 32:13). And Christ, anointed of God,
is the oil of healing for every bruise and wound, and the
oil of gladness for every sorrow.

When Zechariah calls Jesus a "stone," he is in agreement
with others who state the same truth. Isaiah calls him "a
tried stone," "a precious corner stone," and "a sure foundation" (28:16). The psalmist said: "The stone which the
builders refused is become the head stone of the corner"
(118:22).

Paul, the great Aristotle and Demosthenes of the Jewish
race, the great apostle who left a trail of glory across the
Gentile world, says:

Now therefore ye are no more strangers and foreign-
ers, but fellowcitizens with the saints, and of the

household of God; and are built upon the foundation
of the apostles and prophets, Jesus Christ himself
being the chief corner stone; in whom all the building
fitly framed together groweth unto an holy temple
in the Lord: in whom ye also are builded together
for an habitation of God through the Spirit
(Eph. 2:19-22).

Edward Mote sang:

"On Christ the solid Rock I stand;
All other ground is sinking sand.

....

When darkness seems to hide his face;
I rest on His unchanging grace."

And here, in our text, Jesus and the use of Jesus is
announced. "He is the basis to sustain the complete salvation of the church of God, which is his home—his temple."
Of such a structure how great would be the fall! The crash
would be heard beyond the stars. But who—or what—can
bear up the weight of such an edifice? We? No. Our
worthiness? No. Our wisdom? No. Our philosophies? No.
Our works? No. Our righteousness? No. Our strength? No.
More easily could the quicksands of the marsh support
the skyscrapers of Manhattan. More surely could the frag-
ile leaf of autumn support the pillars of the earth. More
surely could a baby's dimpled hand take a toy hammer
and pound the pyramids to dust. But Jesus who holds this
world in the hands of his omnipotence is infinitely equal
to the importance of this station—and "whosoever believeth
on him shall not be ashamed" (Rom. 9:33).

Yes, the living Word of our living God stars Jesus. All
the Bible's analogies, types, pictures, and truths are so
related to Christ that Christ alone explains them. And the

explanation is filled with such perfection of harmony in every detail, the relationship between them and our Lord Jesus is so strikingly self-evident that further discussion would be to light lamps at noonday.

This text is rich in meaning. While most interesting are the visions found in the first six chapters of a symbolical character—most interesting also is the fact that Zechariah makes Jesus the cynosure of all eyes. Most gripping it is to notice that the last six chapters of his prophecy "predict" Alexander's expedition along the west coast of Palestine to Egypt; God's protection of the Jews, both at the time and under the Maccabees; the advent, sufferings, and reign of Messiah; the destruction of Jerusalem by Rome and the dissolution of the Jews' polity; their restoration; the overthrow of the wicked confederacy which assailed them in Canaan, and the Gentiles' joining in their holy worship—but still more importantly gripping is the antitypical truth that the foundation stone alluded to is Christ, before called the Branch, and that Jesus is to be seen of all see-ers, the observed of all observers, the scrutinized of all scrutinizers, the examined of all examiners! Yes; and that as surely as in the days of his flesh "the eyes of all them that were in the synagogue were fastened on him" (Luke 4:20)—as certainly as the psalmist says, "The eyes of all wait upon thee" (145:15).

The words of our text call attention to the notice, the observation, that Jesus was to excite and engage—Jesus whose life on this earth was an episode between two eternities, one reaching back before all worlds, the other forward forever. Verily, Jesus was to be the observed of earthly hosts, the observed of heavenly hosts, of hellish hosts—the looked-upon one by all lookers. "Upon one

stone shall be seven eyes." *Seven* here does not mean
merely seven—seven apples or seven soldiers—but a perfect
number. Just as the eye is the symbol of Providence, so
it is, too, of perfection. The following verses bear out this
teaching.

"And I beheld, and, lo, in the midst of the throne,
and of the four beasts, and in the midst of the elders,
stood a Lamb as it had been slain, having seven horns
and seven eyes, which are the seven Spirits of God
sent forth into all the earth" (Rev. 5:6).

"For the eyes of the Lord run to and fro throughout
the whole earth, to shew himself strong in behalf of
them whose heart is perfect toward him. Herein thou
hast done foolishly; therefore from henceforth thou
shalt have wars" (2 Chron. 16:9).

"I will instruct thee and teach thee in the way which
thou shalt go: I will guide thee with mine eye"
(Ps. 32:8).

Jesus is "a living stone"—and, as to his own sevenfold
perfection, "full of eyes of perfect intelligence, who not
only attracts the eyes of multitudes, but emits illumination
so as to direct them to Him." Remembering that God's
definitions and man's definitions are not in the same dic-
tionary, that God's scales and man's scales do not weigh
alike, that God's arithmetic and man's arithmetic are
strangely at variance, we can say that "seven" here is
designed to indicate a great multitude.

"Then came Peter to him, and said, Lord, how oft shall
my brother sin against me, and I forgive him? till seven
times? Jesus saith unto him, I say not unto thee, Until
seven times: but, Until seventy times seven" (Matt. 18:21-
22). But Jesus did not mean merely to be arithmetically

exact and tell Peter he must forgive four hundred and ninety times, but many times beyond four hundred and ninety. And the expression "seven eyes" does not mean merely seven eyes but the eyes of a great multitude.

The Eyes of God Were and Are upon Jesus.

"For the land, whither thou goest in to possess it, is not as the land of Egypt, from which ye came out, where thou sowedst thy seed, and wateredst it with thy feet, as a garden of herbs: but the land, whither ye go to possess it, is a land of hills and valleys, and drinketh water of the rain of heaven: a land which the Lord thy God careth for: the eyes of the Lord thy God are always upon it, from the beginning of the year even unto the end of the year" (Deut. 11:10-12).

Thus is stated the truth of the constantly seeing eyes of God which see the whole land, every corner of it, through every hour of every day, through every minute of every hour of every night.

The perpetually perceiving eyes of God are omnipresent: "The eyes of the Lord are in every place, beholding the evil and the good" (Prov. 15:3).

The eyes of the Lord, which "run to and fro through the whole earth" see all the ways of men: "For the ways of man are before the eyes of the Lord, and he pondereth all his goings" (Prov. 5:21).

There are paths which crocodiles' eyes never see. There are vistas which eagles' eyes cannot scan. There are paths in impenetrable jungles which lions' eyes cannot see. There are trackless paths in the oceans' depths which birds can never see, just as there are storm clouds which the eyes

of ocean monsters never see. There are ant trails which
eyes of sparrows never see, just as there are sparrows'
flights which ants' eyes never see. There are mysterious
roads in the human body which man's microscopic eyes
never see. There are circling planet paths which man's
most far-reaching telescopic eyes never see and cannot
see. There are strange pathways in solid substances which
man's spectographic eyes cannot penetrate. There are roads
which serpents' bellies have never pressed, which serpents'
glittering eyes have never glimpsed. There are blind alleys
which turn out to the scrapheap, the prison, the madhouse
and the grave, which the eyes of many never see. There
are roads which the feet of many have never trod, which
the eyes of many now in their tombs have never seen—such
as the Santa Fe Trail that "bored through the wilderness,
the desert, and the Rocky Mountains into the land of gold,"
such as the Oregon Trail which "crept down the Snake
River to the mouth of the Columbia."

But there have never been paths which God's eyes saw
not. And nowhere are there any trails and roads now which
God's eyes see not. Be it any hill trail in the desert—he
sees. Be it caterpillar's trail in the rose garden—he sees.
Be it a metropolitan highway jammed with traffic—he sees.
Midnight is as the noonday to God's eyes.

"If I say, Surely the darkness shall cover me, even the
night shall be light about me. Yes, the darkness hideth
not from thee; but the night shineth as the day: the darkness and the light are both alike to thee" (Ps. 139:11-12).
He sees all and in all places.

God knew Christ's "gifts of the Spirit."

"And the spirit of the Lord shall rest upon him, the
spirit of wisdom and understanding, the spirit of
counsel and might, the spirit of knowledge and of

the fear of the Lord; and shall make him of quick understanding in the fear of the Lord: and he shall not judge after the sight of his eyes, neither reprove after the hearing of his ears" (Isa. 11:2-3).

God the Father knew the fullness of grace in his own Son. "And of his fulness have all we received, and grace for grace" (John 1:16). "For it pleased the Father that in him should all fulness dwell" (Col. 1:19).

God knew the words that Jesus spoke: "For he whom God hath sent speaketh the words of God: for God giveth not the Spirit by measure unto him" (John 3:34).

And the eyes of the Father ever rested with delight upon him. No finite understanding can conceive the joyful complacency God had in contemplating him—in looking upon him in the glory which Jesus had with God before the world was. "Then I was by him, as one brought up with him: and I was daily his delight, rejoicing always before him" (Prov. 8:30).

God's eyes were upon him when he was wrapped in Bethlehem's swaddling clothes, where he was God's will, God's thought, God's purpose wrapped in mortality. God's eyes were upon him when, held close in his mother's arms, he was carried into Egypt to escape Herod's massacre. God's eyes were upon him when, as a lad of twelve, he confused with his questions the scholars of his day—and confounded them with answers to their questions. There, in answer to his mother's telling of the sorrow which his father and she had in seeking him, Jesus speaks of no father but one, saying in effect, "My Father has not been seeking me; I have been with him all this time." "The king hath brought me into his chambers. . . . His left hand is under my head, and his right hand doth embrace me" (Song of Sol. 1:4; 2:6).

God's eyes were upon him during those years when no record of his life is given. God's eyes were upon him when he toiled in the carpenter shop, when he was buried in baptism in Jordan's singing and sobbing waters, when his eyes were closed in sleep and when flashed in flames of righteous indignation in the Temple courts, when he prayed, when he wrought his miracles. God's eyes were upon him in Gethsemane's garden, in Pilate's court where they seared his quivering flesh with red scars—and on Calvary's bloody cross where God ordered sin to execution in the person of his dear Son. No finite mind can conceive the delight—the painful delight—God had in looking upon him while he was achieving the redemption of his people and finishing the redemptive work which God gave him to do. But always God would say: "Behold my servant, whom I uphold; mine elect, in whom my soul delighteth; I have put my spirit upon him: he shall bring forth judgment to the Gentiles" (Isa. 42:1).

And always God's testimony was: "This is my beloved Son, in whom I am well pleased."

The Eyes of All Angels Are upon Jesus.

"And without controversy great is the mystery of godliness: God was manifested in the flesh, justified in the Spirit, seen of angels, preached unto the Gentiles, believed on in the world, received up into glory" (1 Tim. 3:16).

"Seen of angels." We read of "an innumerable company of angels" (Heb. 12:22). We read of "the sufferings of Christ, and the glory that should follow" and of the gospel preached "with the Holy Ghost sent down from heaven; which things angels desire to look into" (1 Pet. 1:11-12).

Seen of angels! And angels worshiped him (Heb. 1:6)!

Angels—created beings who never become sick, never marry, never sin, never die—worshiped him in the preincarnate glory which he had with God before the world was.

An angel, even Gabriel, announced to Mary, his virgin mother, that she would conceive in her womb, and "bring forth a son, and . . . call his name Jesus" (Luke 1:31). "And when eight days were accomplished for the circumcising of the child, his name was called JESUS, which was so named of the angel before he was conceived in the womb" (Luke 2:21).

Angels caroled at his birth. An angel warned Joseph of his danger because of Herod. "Angels came and ministered unto him" in the wilderness after his terrible temptations. In the garden of Gethsemane, when the weight of the world's sins were in great agonies upon him, "there appeared an angel unto him from heaven, strengthening him" (Luke 22:43).

Twelve legions of angels were ready at his bidding to come to his rescue the night of his arrest. "Thinkest thou that I cannot now pray to my Father, and he shall presently give me more than twelve legions of angels?" (Matt. 26:53).

> "Through all His travels here below
> The angel did His steps attend;
> Oft gazed and wondered where at last,
> The scene of love would end.
>
> "Around the bloody tree
> They pressed with strong desire
> That wondrous sight to see—
> The Lord of Life expire;
> And could their eyes have known a tear,

Had dropped it there, in sad surprise."

When he rose from the dead, an angel had ministry in his resurrection. "And, behold, there was a great earthquake: for the angel of the Lord descended from heaven, and came and rolled back the stone from the door, and sat upon it. His countenance was like lightning, and his raiment white as snow" (Matt. 28:2-3).

And to the fearful women, it was an angel who spoke comfortingly for the record reads: "And the angel answered and said unto the women, Fear not ye: for I know that ye seek Jesus which was crucified. He is not here: for he is risen, as he said. Come, see the place where the Lord lay" (vv. 5-6).

And two angels had words with Mary that resurrection day:

> "But Mary stood without at the sepulchre weeping: and as she wept, she stooped down, and looked into the sepulchre, and seeth two angels in white sitting, the one at the head, and the other at the feet, where the body of Jesus had lain, And they say unto her, Woman, why weepest thou? She saith unto them, Because they have taken away my Lord, and I know not where they have laid him" (John 20:11-13).

And it was an angel Jesus sent to give testimony: "I Jesus sent mine angel to testify unto you these things in the churches. I am the root and the offspring of David, and the bright and morning star" (Rev. 22:16).

And when Jesus comes to earth again—this same Jesus "in like manner as ye have seen him go into heaven" (Acts 1:11)—all his holy angels will be with him (Matt. 25:31).

The Eyes of Satan Were upon Him.

More greedily than eyes of wolf are upon the flock of
sheep to molest, more cruelly than eyes of eagle are upon
the dovecote to rob it, more subtly than eyes of serpent
are upon the sparrow to charm it into captivity, more
persistently than eyes of fox are upon the rabbit to kill
it, more keenly than eyes of archer are upon the pigeon
to bring it to earth—with an arrow in the body, more
eagerly than eyes of hound are upon the stag to bring
it to death, were the eyes of Satan upon Jesus. Ceaselessly
and with devilish determination, Satan watched him
through life. Always, though his plans were oft frustrated,
did Satan hope to make a prey of him, the Second Adam,
as he had done to the first Adam when he brought about,
through the sin of our first parents, the pitching of the
black pavilion of despair upon man's sterile and blasted
estate.

When we read of the first temptation, when Satan tried
to make Jesus turn the stones into bread and thus serve
himself, we see that Satan was a stern reality to Jesus.
When we understand how in the second temptation Satan,
by urging Christ to cast himself down from the pinnacle
of the Temple, said: "Let God serve you," we understand
that Satan was a grim reality to Jesus. When we see how
Satan, after showing him "all the kingdoms of the world,"
sought to get Jesus to avoid the cross by bowing down
to Satan, we know that Satan was a stubborn reality to
Jesus. As to the first temptation Satan said, "Serve yourself," as in the second temptation he said, "Let God serve
you," so in the third temptation, Satan said, "Let me serve
you." And Satan who has brought many heart-born hopes
to nought, who has made many sacred vows fall short

of realization, who has afflicted many hearts with a sense of perjury and self-contempt, who has encircled many with malign power, was determined to thwart Jesus in his purpose of redemptive grace. Jesus never denied the personality of Satan, who is thus described: "And the great dragon was cast out, that old serpent, called the Devil, and Satan, which deceiveth the whole world: he was cast into the earth, and his angels were cast out with him" (Rev. 12:9).

Jesus never doubted Satan's power to deceive, Jesus was never ignorant of Satan's devices, Jesus knew that many were "taken captive by him at his will."

Yes, Satan, whom John called a murderer, a liar, a sinner "from the beginning," whom Peter calls an adversary and a devourer, whom Matthew calls an enemy and a tempter, whom Paul describes as one who "is transformed into an angel of light," was a grim, sometimes ghastly, reality to Jesus.

In Jesus' days of flesh on earth, even as now, Satan had his angels. "The devil and his angels" (Matt. 25:41). He had, even as now, his children: "The children of the devil" (1 John 3:10). He had, even as now he has them, his workers: "He that committeth sin is of the devil; for the devil sinneth from the beginning. For this purpose the Son of God was manifested, that he might destroy the works of the devil" (1 John 3:8). He had, even as now he has them, his snares. "The snare of the devil" (1 Tim. 3:7). He had, even as now he has them, his followers. "For some are already turned aside after Satan" (1 Tim. 5:15). He had, even as now he has them, his wiles. "The wiles of the devil" (Eph. 6:11). He had, even as now he has them, his devices: "Lest Satan should get an advantage of us: for we are not ignorant of his devices" (2 Cor. 2:11). He had, even as now he has it, his power:

"The power of Satan" (Acts 26:18). "The working of Satan with all power" (2 Thess. 2:9).

He had, even as now he has it, his wrath. "The devil is come down unto you, having great wrath" (Rev. 12:12). He had, even as now he has them, his messengers. "The messenger of Satan to buffet me" (2 Cor. 12:7). He had, even as now he has them, his ministers. "Therefore it is no great thing if his ministers also be transformed as the ministers of righteousness; whose end shall be according to their works" (2 Cor. 11:15). And all these he used against Jesus, even as now he uses them against those who would follow Jesus. And when we remember that Satan tried to get Jesus to become an earthly king, tried to turn him aside from his substituting, vicarious, atoning death on the cross, we know that to Satan, life was a battleground—not a playground. We read that Jesus "himself hath suffered being tempted" (Heb. 2:18). "For we have not an high priest which cannot be touched with the feeling of our infirmities; but was in all points tempted like as we are, yet without sin" (4:15).

Thus we see that upon Jesus were the eyes of Satan— Satan who capers with the cultured, fuddles with the fool, frolics with the frivolous, prays with the pious, dances with the devilish, plods with the poor, races with the rich, romps with royalty, vies with the vicious, works with the wicked, trots with the thrill-seekers.

Satan knew the vulnerable spot in Achilles' heel. He caused Adam, the perfect man, to become imperfect. He caught Abraham in his faithfulness and caused him to lie about his beautiful wife. He caught Moses in his meekness and caused him to kill—as he thought the sands in God's hourglass were running too slowly. He allured Samson in his strength and brought him to death. He caught Job

in his patience and caused him to curse the day he was
born. He ensnared David in his insecurity and caused him
foolishly to stake his crown for a woman's caress. He
blinded Solomon in all his glory and made his sun set
at midnight. He caught Elijah in his fearlessness at a time
of physical strain and exhaustion and made him pray to
die. He caught John the Baptist in his greatness and caused
him to question Jesus. He caught Peter in his confidence
and caused him to deny and swear. He caught Thomas
in his willingness to die for Jesus and made him doubt.

But, though his eyes were upon Jesus day and night
and at all places, never did he get Jesus to strike a jarring
note, never to say anything he ought not to have said,
never to leave unsaid anything he ought to have said, never
to have deceit in his mouth, never to pray selfishly, never
to falter in the face of antagonism, never to hurry in the
presence of popular acclaim, never to be betrayed into
an error of judgment, never to become humiliated by a
moral fall. In the Lord of heaven Satan found nothing
wrong—and could get him to do no wrong. Still he asks
as one who can never be answered: "Which of you convic-
teth me of sin?" (John 8:46). Let us rejoice in the truth
of this: "For in that he himself hath suffered being tempted,
he is able to succour them that are tempted" (Heb. 2:18).

The Eyes of the Prophets and Patriarchs Were upon Jesus.

Upon Jesus, the observed of all observers, are—by the
Holy Spirit—the eyes of patriarchs, the eyes of prophets.
Though they did not see Jesus in the flesh as did the chosen
twelve, yet their eyes were upon him—as "the rainbow
of prophecy reaches from Mount Moriah to Calvary."
Abraham in whom the genius of the Jewish race is sum-
marized, in the Scripture called "the friend of God," in

whom "all the nations of the earth shall be blessed"—of him Jesus said: "Your father Abraham rejoiced to see my day: and he saw it, and was glad" (John 8:56).

Old Jacob, whose last days were spent in Egypt as a guest of the most powerful king in the world, whose eyes doubtless saw the tombs in the pyramids "where kings lay buried in coffins hewn from gold," whose eyes doubtless gazed upon the Sphinx with the "sightless orbs of ivory" whose eyes saw "the temples whose gravity columns overwhelm us even unto this day," had his eyes upon Jesus when, as he lay and his sons knelt at his side, he said: "The sceptre shall not depart from Judah, nor a lawgiver from between his feet, until Shiloh comes; and unto him shall the gathering of the people be" (Gen. 49:10).

That mysterious utterance from Jacob's death-cooled lips burns forth into immortal music in the singing of the angels over the hills of Bethlehem—after the roll of centuries.

One day to King Pharaoh, the incarnation of Oriental tyranny, came Moses, the Jewish ambassador of Jehovah, "born under the shadow of the pyramids," more gigantic than the pyramids, saying: "God of the Hebrews hath sent me unto thee, saying, Let my people go." Led by Moses, the people did go forth—as God "brought out that he might bring them in," and for them by the direction of God, Moses formulated a ceremonial system which expressed faith in God, sacrifice for sin, atonement and prayer for reconciliation. Those diversified and systematic sacrifices were significant shadows of redemptive entity still ahead, adumbrations of a substance yet to come—elemental, preparatory, rudimentary, introductory—pointing to Christ the propellant center to which the faith of mankind gravitated. All the moral elements of the entire ceremonial system made for Christ's crucifixion a vivid background, and Jesus himself said: "Do not think that I will accuse you to the Father, there is one that accuseth you, even Moses, in whom ye trust. For had ye believed Moses, ye would have believed me: for he wrote of me" (John 5:45-46).

David, speaking the language of the universal emotion, knowing how to wear the purple, knowing how to grasp the scepter, "the embodiment of his nation's qualities, the incarnation of his nation's spirit, the type of his nation's destiny," wrote the Psalms—the Psalms that glow like living coals. "The satire of Horace, the invective of Juvenal, the sublimity of Homer, the solemnity of Dante, the tragic verse of Shakespeare—all these attributes belong to his genius." But consider how often whether "joy hours that make the mountains luminous" or in the imprecatory Psalms, "when the storm spirit puts forth the forest to its lips and blows a trumpet blast of anger." David's verses are filled with prophecies of the Messiah,

Job, voicing the anguish of generations, reflecting the heartcries of centuries, asking God questions through lips festering with disease, pleading in dense darkness for light, gazing into the future hearing doubtless, amid the whirlwind that stifled him, the voice of Christ, and seeing "afar off in the centuries a cross tilted," said, his eyes upon Jesus, "I know that my redeemer liveth."

Study Elijah, tawny with the burning suns of Palestine, stouthearted and thunder-voiced, with an anger that blazed like the wrath of Achilles, fire and hail and stormy wind authenticating his divine mission, a union of the terrible with the gentle, calling an apostate nation back to God.

Consider Elisha, wrapped in an aura of profoundest spiritual truth, the honored mouthpiece of God at the court of six kings, miracles without number credited to him, anticipating more than Elijah the spirit of Jesus Christ.

Think of Joel—at a time when locusts cursed the earth, he asked people to rend their hearts and not their garments—asked for a day of national humiliation and prayer—foresaw God's Spirit being poured upon all flesh.

Remember Jonah. Behind the curtain of his fearless preaching, old Nineveh, once gay and giddy, strutting and sinful, no longer shook defiant fists, but bent humble knees.

Give thought to Amos, the soul of fury. He impeached civilizations, summoned the nations to judgment. At a time when the outside of the cup was polished, the inside tarnished and foul, "his eyes and lips threw flame as he condemned Damascus for cruelty, Gaza for torturing slaves, Tyre for voluptuousness, Edom for savage lust, Moab for scarlet vice, and Israel for using the temple of idolatry for a winding sheet around Jehovah's altars."

Consider Hosea, prophet of love, the essence of tenderness, addressing the heart—adding consolation to condemnation and complaint. No wonder someone said that to understand the gospel of Jesus, his view of God, his love of mankind, one should read Hosea.

Think of Isaiah, prophet of royalty, prophet of the city, prophet of world kingdoms, the first evangelist among the prophets—whose prophecy about Jesus reads more like history than prophecy. In all his preaching was the growl of the Assyrian wolf (the weapon of judgment). He had the vision of the Messiah—and said that the Messiah's name should be called "wonderful" and "Counselor," and "the mighty God" and "the everlasting Father" and "the Prince of peace"—upon whose shoulders shall be the government.

Think of Nahum, seeing afar the chariots of the Medes,

unrolling the centuries, revealing the Messiah. "Behold upon the mountains the feet of him that bringeth good tidings."

See Habakkuk. He saw Nineveh fall to Babylon, saw the Chaldean become a crueler tyrant over Judah than the Assyrians. But he believed that the earth would "be filled with the knowledge of the glory of the Lord, as the waters cover the sea."

Time would fail me to tell of Zephaniah, wailing that false worshipers, waverers, apostates had "knit well the threads of doom on a loom of evil destiny"; of Obadiah—talking of the coming vengeance on the whole race; of Jeremiah—his weeping something like the weeping of an archangel over a lost world; of Daniel, prophesying that the Messiah would be an interblending of heavenly and earthly nature; of Ezekiel, using coffins for a text, eating filth to describe the horrors of slavery, "whose tears turn to blood as he listens to the rumbling wheels of oncoming judgment"; of Haggai—exhorter, enthusiast, his one text "Build the Temple"; of Zephaniah, laboring with "his fiery judgments fretted with golden mercies"; of Malachi, standing in "the falling dusk of a night that was to be four hundred years long," yet seeing the dawn in which walks the Son of man. Which is to say, as we look upon this parade of prophets, that the prophets "horoscoped the personality of the Messiah." Which is to say that the prophets and Christ belong together. Which is to say that, as is affirmed by the Christian scholarship of twenty centuries, the prophecies of the Old Testament culminate in Jesus Christ. Upon this living stone were the eyes of the prophets.

"Then he said unto them, O fools, and slow of heart to believe all that the prophets have spoken: ought

not Christ to have suffered these things and to enter
into his glory?" (Luke 24:25-26).

The Eyes of Men Were upon Jesus.

Men fastened their eyes scrutinizingly upon him as
physicists with their microscopic lenses observe the crea-
tures in a drop of water. Men looked observingly upon
him as astronomers, with their telescopes, studied distant
worlds.

Pious Joseph of Nazareth, marveling with Mary at her
Son, passing the habit of hard labor to the Son apprenticed
at his side, looked upon him in adoration—wondering
daily.

Aged Simeon, promised a glimpse of the coming Messiah before he died, with glistening eyes and heart aburst,
saw him and wished to see nobody else and nothing else,
and said, "Lord, now lettest thy servant depart in peace."

The shepherds saw him, "and they came with haste,
and found Mary, and Joseph, and the babe lying in a
manger. . . . And the shepherds returned glorifying and
praising God for all the things that they had heard and
seen, as it was told unto them" (Luke 2:16,20).

The Wise Men saw him, "and when they were come
into the house, they saw the young child with Mary his
mother, and fell down and worshipped him: and when
they had opened their treasures, they presented unto him
gifts; gold, and frankincense, and myrrh" (Matt. 2:11).

John the Baptist, "the morning star of the kingdom of
God, a voice crying in the wilderness, clearing the way
for the Conqueror," saw him and said, "He must increase,
but I must decrease."

Blind Bartimaeus, "crouching by the highway down
which came the pilgrims to the Passover," hearing with

keen ears what he could not see with dead eyes, saw Jesus
after he had healed him. Bartimaeus never squatted in
the dust again; he followed Christ.

The wild man of Gadara, ghastly with his self-inflicted
wounds, making the night hideous with his insane cries,
saw him—and never wanted to leave him.

Zacchaeus, little of stature, rich in purse, greedy of heart,
sick of conscience, unsatisfied of heart, a taxgathering
Shylock, a pitiless profiteer, saw Jesus—and, after Jesus,
behind closed doors of Zacchaeus' house, had brought him
to penitence and salvation, he wanted to make restitution
fourfold of all he had stolen.

Judas, "the hiss of a serpent hidden in his name," saw
him for three years—at weddings, in rooms of death, in
private, in public, among enemies, among friends—saw him
closely—and confessed before he hanged himself, that he
had betrayed the innocent One.

Wavering Pilate, afraid of committing an injustice, afraid
to do justice, saw him judicially and said, "I am innocent
of the blood of this just person. I find no fault in this
man."

Of the centurion, who supervised the bloody butchery
on the cross, who watched him in death, we have this
record: "Now when the centurion, and they that were with
him, watching Jesus, saw the earthquake, and those things
that were done, they feared greatly, saying, Truly this was
the Son of God" (Matt. 27:54).

Acquaintances and women from Galilee saw him. The
record is: "And all his acquaintances, and the women that
followed him from Galilee, stood afar off, beholding these
things" (Luke 23:49).

And many others saw him. For 'tis said: "And all the
people that came together to that sight, beholding the

things which were done, smote their breasts, and returned" (Luke 23:48).

Mary, his mother, standing by the cross, saw him in his life often—saw him, too, in death. "Now there stood by the cross of Jesus his mother" (John 19:25). And what her emotions were when she viewed the head, which had oft reposed on her bosom, fall lifeless, I cannot describe.

The disciples, oft in synagogue, oft in the Temple, oft on highways, often in the storms, often in the midst of disease, oft in the presence of hostile enemies, saw him. They saw him also after the resurrection: "And when he had so said, he shewed unto them his hands and his side. Then were the disciples glad, when they saw the Lord" (John 20:20).

And Paul says: "Have not I seen Jesus Christ?"—Yes—and even at midday, Jesus shone above the brightness of the sun.

And let us not forget that millions since the crucifixion have seen him. How? With eyes of the body? No. But with the eyes of the mind. How? With the eyes of sense? No. But with the eyes of faith. Indeed this is the great essential. "And this is the will of him that sent me, that every one which seeth the Son, and believeth on him, may have everlasting life: I will raise him up at the last day" (John 6:40).

Recalling these words, we need to remember that the one aim of the gospel and all the ordinances of religion is to focus the eyes of men on him. There is no hope in any other. There is no salvation in any other. He, therefore, cries, Behold me! Behold me! "Look unto me, and be ye saved, all the ends of the earth: for I am God, and there is none else" (Isa. 45:22).

Every true minister endeavors to awaken attention to

Jesus and with John the Baptist: "Behold the Lamb of God,
which taketh away the sin of the world!" Behold Jesus!
"Look unto me, and be ye saved!" This is God's invitation
to all men everywhere. He invites you to look upon him
and be saved. If you look upon yourself, you will see your
own sins—and they are many! If you look to others, you
will see their sins—and they are grievous. If you look at
modern examples, you will be disappointed—as men who
seek to keep clothes white in coal mines. If you look to
the worldly-wise for guidance, you will go wrong. "The
arm of flesh will fail you." But nobody goes wrong if he
goes in the direction Jesus indicates, if he follows the road
Jesus travels.

'Tis said that more eyes are not upon him. But more
are viewing him than you are aware of. Someday many
Jews with eyes of faith will look upon him whom they
have pierced. Gentiles shall come to his light, and kings
to the brightness of his rising. Yes, all nations shall serve
him. Yea, all kings shall fall down before him.

"Wherefore God also hath highly exalted him, and
given him a name which is above every name: that
at the name of Jesus every knee should bow, of things
in heaven, and things in earth and things under the
earth" (Phil. 2:9-10).

In Another World Many Eyes Shall Be upon Jesus.

"And they shall see his face; and his name shall be
in their foreheads" (Rev. 22:4). In the tearless, fearless
world, he is all in all. There he draws every eye. There
he employs every tongue. There his servants shall serve
him. There his servants shall see his face. There his name
shall be in their foreheads. "Beloved, now are we the sons

of God, and it doth not yet appear what we shall be: but we know that, when he shall appear, we shall be like him; for we shall see him as he is" (1 John 3:2).

If I miss that time and heaven, how utterly worthless will be everything else that I have called my own! My mother, who since my baby days spoke to me of God, and who sent me her blessing from her deathbed, is in heaven. My father, who stands before me today as old Samuel of Gilgal, as honest a man as any man ever knew, one who would suffer his right arm to be cut off before he would cheat a man or refuse to pay a debt he owed, and whose dying breath was like the last whisper of a storm that spent itself, is in heaven. Many of the dearest friends I have, men and women for whom I would have died and who would have as willingly died for me, are in heaven.

What will making a fortune amount to—if I miss heaven? What will gaining a bit more temporary applause be worth—if I miss heaven? What will a little more luxurious comfort amount to—if I miss heaven? How can the gain of the world repay me for the loss of heaven? What but beggarly rags, what but cold ashes, what but trash, what but tawdry pearls of paste are all earthly things compared with the hope of heaven and the meeting there in eternal reunion and fellowship with those who, redeemed by Christ's blood, have reached the other side of "death's cold, sullen stream"? We can miss money—if we must. We can miss worldly success—if we must. We can miss honor and praise—if we must. We can endure hardness—if we must. We can have crushing burdens—if we must. But we must not miss heaven where, for "ten thousand times ten thousand years, bright shining as the sun," we shall see him of whom Zechariah spoke (Zech. 3:9).

3.
The Saving Name of Jesus

The angel appeared to Joseph in the long ago while Mary was with child of the Holy Ghost and said: "Thou shalt call his name JESUS: for he shall save his people from their sins" (Matt. 1:21).

There are names that give courage to warriors' hearts, names that give inspiration to philosophers' minds—names that give skill to sculptors' chisels, glory to painters' canvases, earnestness to teachers' arguments, fire to poets' frenzy, eloquence to orators' utterances, immortality to lovers' songs, endurance to athletes' struggles, joy to martyrs' sufferings, sacredness to marital relationships, power to writers' pens.

There is a name that gives strength to friendship when the road is rough—and there are more thorns to endure than roses to kiss. There is a name that is a roof and refuge when "the storm is up and all is on the hazard"—when heavens thunder and fire roams the sky. There is a name that is warmth when the visiting bywords of criticism howl, "Cold strengthens as days lengthen." There is a name that is light when "all around is darkness like a wall." There is a name that stimulates when men, "stretched on the cushions of a too-easy chair," "with yarns confess the pain and penalties of idleness."

There is a name that gives wisdom when men are talkative and fierce with their tongues, gives courage when men are timid with their hearts and hands. There is a name that gives rebuke to the slothful "whose fat blood sleeps as it creeps along their veins." There is a name that is liberty when evil habits hamper one's effort as ice on a bird's wings hinders its flight. There is a name that is a bondage-breaking name for those bound "with links of shame more strong than iron and more keen than flame."

'Tis the name of Jesus—who is from above and is above all. Jesus—the name forever bright with the spiritual incandescence of heaven—like the light of the glory of God in his face. Jesus—the name forever fresher than the "pure river . . . clear as crystal, proceeding out of the throne of God and of the Lamb." Jesus—the name luminous like the city whose light is the Lamb. Jesus—"sweetest name on mortal tongue," the name of him "with whom no mortal can compare." Jesus!

Can musicians who build rhythmic palaces of melody before the eyes of men's souls create melody compared with the name of Jesus? No. Can the fields furnish flowers with sweetness or the sunrise skies glow with splendor or the midnight exhibit stars compared with the name of Jesus? Botanists and painters and astronomers and prophets say no. Truly men speak words of sober joy and truth when they declare that the loveliest beauty and the most beautiful loveliness have no splendor compared with the name of Jesus.

In that Name alone, sinners find heaven's grace for earth's guilt. In that Name above every name, transgressors find heaven's glory for earth's shame and heaven's pardon for earth's perversities. In that Name alone, the grief-stricken find comfort for suffocating sorrows—until "sorrow and sighing shall flee away." In that Name alone men find the protection of truth when men falsely "speak unto us smooth things and prophesy deceits."

In that Name alone men find chart and compass when the mind is thrown upon futurity and there "finds a vast ocean where men are wearied with winds and waves." In that Name alone men find sufficient strength and wisdom when to be weak is to be wretched and when men "exceed in folly all fools that are, have been, or shall be." In that Name alone is heaven's water for men's thirst when "wasting and a new troop of fevers has settled upon the earth."

In that Name alone is heaven's brightest hope for earth's ghastliest death, heaven's most glorious glory for earth's blackest shame, heaven's potently promised and guaranteed resurrection for earth's darkest tomb.

Jesus—Name Possessing Wealth of Sublime Simplicity

Not a name that entangles men's tongues or presents perplexities or hesitancy in pronunciation. Though Jesus is the overtopping character of all time, his name is not difficult of pronunciation—like Artaxerxes, Belteshenesh, Chermonesus, Nebuchadnezzar. Though musicians who "make surging seas of tone subservient to their rods" testify in music to the glory of his name—yet "his voice has more music in it than is to be heard in all the oratorios of eternity"—and his name so pleasingly pronounceable is ceaseless music at the throne which overlooks the world.

Though sculptors testify that he is the most graceful symmetry in all sculpture and that they can in no quarry find marble white enough for his brow, yet his is no name that makes us listen with sharp intensity. Though orators whose words are flights of golden arrows testify that truths he taught are the brightest gems in their grandest flights, yet the two-syllable name—Jesus—is the dome of all vocal grandeur—the peroration of all splendid language; and the prattling child does not have to hear that name several times before he ventures to speak it. For that name fits the tongue of the babe learning to talk, as well as the tongue of the orator to whom people listen like slaves to an emancipation proclamation.

From the tongues of mothers singing lullabies to their children and from the tongues of choirs with tenor triumphs and soprano superlatives and alto excellence and bass blessedness of song that name falls with ease. And when old age, sometimes beset with incessant woes, draws nigh to the sunset gates with voice that speaks feebly, tremblingly, and indistinctly, still the name Jesus is the weightiest and sweetest word when they sing:

> "Jesus, I love Thy charming name,
>   'Tis music to my ear;
> Fain would I sound it out so loud
>   That heaven and earth might hear."

No school is able to express the reach of the name of Jesus who was not stamped with the imprint of the schools, who exhibited no diplomas from the Sanhedrin, who had never visited Athens, the intellectual center of the world, yet said: "Learn of me"—and to whom Peter said: "Thou hast the words of eternal life."

No crown can ever express the royalty of the name of him who loves sinners and washes them from their sins in his own blood and makes them kings and priests unto God—though his only crown was a crown of thorns. No palace of earth is able to show the wealth of the name of Jesus who for our sakes became poor that we through his poverty might become rich, though on earth he was homeless and bedless and pillowless, where foxes had holes and the birds of the air had nests. No scepter is able to set forth the power of the name of Jesus who, though he were the Son of God, "learned . . . obedience by the things which he suffered." No triumphal procession is able to express his triumphant march through the stormy corridors of the centuries—proclaiming victories over sin, death, hell, the grave. And all vocabularies have a woeful sense of inadequacy to oppress them as they try to express with sufficient adequacy the great love of Jesus whose name is the accepted symbol of an atonement coextensive with sin.

And this One whose name is Jesus also said: "I am Alpha and Omega." Thus he appropriated to himself and to his Name all the splendors the greatest thinkers and writers can spell out with those two letters of the Greek alphabet and all the letters between them. "He that cometh from heaven is above all." What does that mean? It means that Jesus is the peerless One with the peerless Name. It means that after you have piled as high as an Alpine peak all the noted names of earth, "the glory of the name of Jesus would have to spread its wings and descend one thousand leagues to touch the summit." Man did not give that name. Man could not give that name. No man can give us one name which, in this connection, deserves to be heard.

True, other names abounded and were mighty when the words were spoken: "Thou shalt call his name Jesus." There was Baal in the east. There was Jupiter in the west. And all their correlative hosts. Even so now, other names abound—and are mighty. Paganism has Buddha, Brahma, and their innumerable subordinates. Magianism and Muhammadanism cling to the fire-priest and sword-prophet. Judaism remembers Moses and hopes for the unrevealed Messiah. But to Jesus, God hath given "a name which is above every name."

Mythology tells us that when the giants warred against the gods, they piled up three mountains—Pelion, Ossa, Olympus—and from the top of them proposed to scale the heavens. But the height was not great enough—and there was complete failure. T. Dewitt Talmage, I believe, referred to that in connection with the name of Jesus, saying: "After all the giants, Isaiah and Paul—prophetical and apostolic giants; Raphael and Michelangelo—artistic giants; David and Shakespeare and Browning—poetical giants; Beethoven and Mendelssohn—musical giants; cherubim and seraphim and archangel—celestial giants; Moses and Grady and Spurgeon—oratorical giants; yea— after all these have failed to climb to the top of Christ's glory, they can unite in saying: 'He that cometh from above is above all.' "

Jesus—Name Possessed of the Wealth of Beauty

We associate names with the persons who have those names. A man's name is not like a mantle, but a perfectly fitting garment. Repulsive as serpents in kindergartens are some names. Hideous as crocodiles in garden pools are some names. Raucous as fussy crows and screeching jays is the mention and remembrance of some names—when we speak of them.

"A great name without merit is like an epitaph on a coffin." Mention Jezebel! You think of one whose life was terrible, whose death was horrible. Mention Athaliah! You think of a woman who was bold and bad, who broke people on the wheel of her unflinching will. Mention Delilah! You think of one in whose heart was the viperous treachery which led Samson to blindness, bonds, and death. Mention Cleopatra! You think of the beautiful adder coiled upon the throne of the Ptolemies who made a wreck of Antony. Mention Madame de Pompadour! You think of the infamous favorite of the court of Louis XV—a woman whose shameless prodigality makes the cheeks of decency burn. Mention Aspasia! You think of the immoral woman who counted Socrates and Pericles among her long list of lovers.

Mention Nero! Your heart has a sudden revolt against his beastly brutality. Mention Absalom! You think of a young man physically without blemish—a wolf in angel's clothes—whose face hid the soul of a devil. Mention Napoleon! You think of him, "the archangel of war," who hurled an avalanche of armies over Europe, who died "a chained Prometheus, the world exultant at his fall." Mention Judas! You think of the pitiful wretch who betrayed divinity, disgraced humanity, and destroyed himself.

Many are the names we never like to hear. Mere mention of the names of some men and women would cause angelic beings to shudder to the tips of their wings. But there are names attractive and sweet to us. While there are persons whose names make you think of vinegar—because they are sour of nature and snappish of tongue, still there are names that are like fragrance to our nostrils, music to our ears, honey to our palates, velvet to our touch, beauty to our eyes.

Mention Jenny Lind! And some recall hearing her sing—feeling yet the thrill of her brilliant, sympathetic soprano voice. Mention Lincoln! In eternity many re-

member with exultant joy the hour in which they grasped
Lincoln's hand, the hand of him whose heart was big as
the world, yet had no room for the memory of a wrong.
Mention Florence Nightingale—and you are grateful for
a marvelous woman who bandaged the world's battle
wounds. Mention Elizabeth Prentiss—and we feel like
singing the lovely hymn she wrote: "More Love to Thee,
O Christ."

So interminably, as one who shovels snowdrifts with
a teaspoon, could we associate names with the persons
holding those names. And that consideration makes Jesus'
name so rich with beauty. And something akin to the
gratitude of Raphael stirs man's soul. "I thank God," said
the painter of *The Transfiguration* "that I live in the time
of Michelangelo."

Say Jesus! You think of Bethlehem where heaven put
out its brightest star to mark his birthplace, where a babe,
ages older than his mother, bent the datelines of all the
nations around his manger cradle. Say Jesus! You think
of Cana of Galilee where at a wedding "the unconscious
water saw its God and blushed." Say Jesus and you think
of Nazareth, with his voluntary poverty, lowly associations,
his subjection to Mary and Joseph, though heaven and
earth gave instant submission to his commands.

Say Jesus! You think of Lake Galilee where you hear
the neighing of a great storm as its comes on with massive
strides like a wild Pegasus in his untamed flight—where
you see the storm kneeling at Jesus' feet and the tempests
folding their wings in Jesus' presence while the "extinguished stars re-light their torches." Again you think of
Galilee, all a-churn with stormy billows—roaring and
heaving and dashing, and of him who walked on the sea—at
the waving of whose hand the wind forbears to blow, and

at the touch of whose footstep the wild waters are calm.

Say Jesus! You think of Bethany where, at the tomb of Lazarus, the tears of humanity streamed from His eyes and the voice of divinity issued from His lips, and awoke the dead to life.

Say Jesus! You think of him as a teacher who rebuked religious leaders for making the Temple a monument of emptiness, or a place for hypocritical seclusion of fraud.

Say Jesus! You think of his miracles—merciful reliefs of old women, widows, children, cures of servants, beggars, lepers, demoniacs—as, looking back to the days of his flesh, you see many rise from their pallets of fever and pain.

Say Jesus! You think of him who was called, to his very face, a bastard, a blasphemer, a glutton, a drunkard, a devil, and yet took no vengeance.

Say Jesus! You see the face more marred than any man's, a face whose cheeks he gave to them who plucked off the hair. Say Jesus! You hear the voice that had in it the gentleness of the zephyr and the force of the cyclone. Say Jesus! You somehow feel the tender touch of him who touched lepers into cleanness, blind eyes into seeing, dumb tongues into singing, deaf ears into hearing, withered hands into wholeness, crippled feet into nimbleness.

Say Jesus! You think of that lonely man who never took a step, or lifted a finger or breathed a word, to injure anyone, but who welcomed to his love the most neglected of the outcast, and poorest of the poor, the dullest of the dull, the vilest of the vile, the saddest of the sad, making his name aromatic with all odors and accordant with all harmonies.

Say Jesus and you think of Gethsemane—where the roots of his divine emotion put forth their crimson tears. Say Jesus and you think of Pilate's judgment hall where they seamed his quivering flesh until it started up in red scars. Say Jesus and you think of Calvary where all the hatreds of men and all the furies of hell charged upon him until there was left no power in bramble or nail or scourge or spear to hurt the dead Son of God.

Say Jesus and you think of the tomb in Joseph's garden where for the first time in thirty-three years the cruel world left him alone. Say Jesus! You think of that resurrection morning when he smashed death's empire of skulls and skeletons with one blow, making the morning glory unfold upon the doorposts of every sepulchre. Say Jesus! You think of Olivet with its sweet farewell memories where, with the clouds as his chariot and the winds as his steeds, he ascended to the Father's right hand—the crowned One of heaven, the Giver of the Holy Ghost. Say Jesus! You think of him who ever liveth to make intercession for us.

Jesus! Only two syllables in that precious name. Yet millions of Chrysostoms and Spurgeons might exhaust their eloquence in trying to express its fullness—and their utmost efforts would be like the breathing of a single breath to show the fullness of the atmosphere. Millions of Mullins and Beechers and Carrolls might exhaust their learning in trying to declare its wonderful wonders—and their best efforts would be as man's mean paint on God's fair lilies. Millions of Savonarolas and Billy Sundays and D. L. Moodys might exhaust their zeal in trying to enforce its spirit—and all their exhortations would prove like the kindling of a taper to illustrate the sunshine.

Millions of Jenny Linds and Carusos might lift their voices in song along with a million others trying to set forth the power of Jesus' name—and all their endeavors would be as a pressure of the hand against a mountain to increase the power of universal gravitation. Millions of musicians—like Timotheus who, with wondrous harmony, subdued the riotous Alexander, like David who drew from his harp a concord that dispelled the gloom from Saul's brow and drove the devils from his heart, like Cecilia who sang until angels were fascinated and men were enraptured, like Eleanor's troubadours at Antioch who bewitched the Syrian air with the ballads of the South—could give their last full measure of musical power to express the full sweetness of his name; and all their manifested musical power would be as the breath of one man's nostrils to express the force of a hurricane, as the blooming of one rose to express the glory and hold the fragrance of one thousand gardens, as the blowing of a tin whistle to produce an oratorio.

"Thou shalt call his name JESUS." Not a name of multitudinous syllables causing the tongue to struggle to pronounce it. But just two syllables. Yet I see gleaming through those two syllables bright tears—worlds of love more wonderful than star worlds brought into view by man's telescopes. If you have ears to hear, the two quiet syllables are stormy with the sighs of Gethsemane and the groans of Calvary. Two syllables—yet reservoirs filled with bitter tears and with holy blood. The two syllables that frame that name sometimes tremble with pain and prayer—sometimes are "a-ripple with gladness and a-ring with hosannas." To invalids on couches of pain—a comfortingly beautiful name. To those bowed with many burdens—a stouteningly beautiful name. To little children filled with laughter and play—a beautiful name. To those who, bowed with burdens, struggle to reach the end of the way—a name replete with comfort.

Jesus—a Name Possessed of the Wealth of Power

Power to save—and power to comfort. "By what power, or by what name have ye done this? By the name of Jesus

Christ of Nazareth" (Acts 4:7,10). The disciples to Jesus:
"The devils are subject through thy name." "In my name
shall they cast out devils." "His name, through faith in
his name hath made this man strong" (Acts 3:16).

"To him give all the prophets witness, that through
his name whosoever believeth in him shall receive
remission of sins" (Acts 10:43).

"And his name through faith in his name hath made
this man strong, whom ye see and know: yea, the
faith which is by him hath given him this perfect
soundness in the presence of you all" (Acts 3:16).

Possessed of power is the name of Rockefeller in the
financial world, the name of Ford in the industrial world,
the name of Edison in the scientific world, the name of
Churchill in the statesmanship world, the name of Shakespeare in the literary world, the name of Jenner and Koch
in the medical world, the name of Thorp and Musial in
the athletic world, the name of Blackstone in the law world,
the name of Washington in the political world, the name
of MacArthur in the military world, the name of Mozart
in the musical world, the name of Michelangelo in the
sculptural world, the name of Millet in the art world, the
name of Socrates in the philosophical world, Peabody in
the philanthropical world, the name of Tennyson in the
poetic world, the name of Clemens in the humor world.
But what name, or cluster of names, is so mighty to inspire
and lift and awe and thrill and arouse and bless and save
as the name of Jesus? "Thou art great, and thy name is
great in might" (Jer. 10:6).

That name Jesus, through faith in that name, made the
apostle Paul more than a conqueror in life and in death
and enabled him to compass the earth with the truths of

redemption. That name, through faith in his name, "flung Newton, the blaspheming infidel, on his face in repentance and faith on the ship's deck." That name, through faith in his name, lifted Mel Trotter out of the horrible pit and out of the miry clay and put his feet on the solid rock and established his going and replaced the song of the drunkard in his mouth with the song of the redeemed. That name, through faith in his name, set the soul of Moody on fire and made him strong to take two continents, the one in his right hand and the other in his left hand, and rock them both toward God. That name, through faith in his name, caught Jerry McCauley, the river wharf thief, and brought him out of bondage into liberty. That name, through faith in his name, drew Rodney Smith, the Gypsy lad—and he followed on, "glad to obey the voice divine." That name, through faith in his name, saved Livingstone, the weaver lad, and sent him to darkest Africa where he opened that highway, marked today by the tombstones of martyred missionaries. That name, through faith in his name, has brought many out of their bondage, sorrow, and night into Christ's freedom, gladness, and light. And time would fail me to tell of others who have like testimony.

"Neither is there salvation in any other: for there is none other name under heaven given among men, whereby we must be saved" (Acts 4:12). *Saved!* From what? From sin and all that sin brings to pass. Sin has ruined men, ruined women, ruined angels. Sin has occasioned every tear of sorrow, every sigh of grief, every pang of agony. Sin has withered everything that is fair, blasted everything that is good, made bitter everything that is sweet, dried up springs of comfort, rolled far and wide tides of sorrow. Sin has digged every grave, built every coffin, woven every shroud, enlarged every cemetery, tied every bit of crepe the world has ever seen.

His is the only saving Name. His is the Name God hath given—given to me, given to you, given to all men under heaven, given it as the Name whereby we may "be saved."

Frank I. Stanton wrote:

"The rain beat on my window pane;
I said, Come in, O rain, O rain;
Come in out of the dark, deep night,
And wash my soul and make it white.
        But the rain replied,
        For the soul that died
        There is only One, the Crucified.

"The wind beat on my window pane,
I said, Come in, O wind, O wind;
Come in out of the wild stormy night
And waft my soul to realms of light.
        But the wind replied,
        For the soul that died
        There is only One, the Crucified."

To these two verses, Dr. I. E. Barton of Montgomery, Alabama, added another:

"The blood beat on my window pane,
I said, Come in, O blood, O blood;
The blood came in from Calvary's night,
And washed my soul and made it white.
        And the blood replied,
        For the soul that died,
        I am thine own, the Crucified."

There is none other name—not even one. *So given*—by the same authority and with the same object. Under heaven—the most expanded comprehension which it is possible to make.

It has been said that "the world is ruled by names." And these names are not without power. But sin is in them—in all its elements, forms, degrees. And, therefore, evil is in them, as the consequence of sin—in all its elements, forms, degrees. But—*salvation* from sin and evil is *not* in them. Yet there is another name, a sweetly holy name, a name above every name, an eternally saving name—for sinful men. Though Baal and Jupiter fail sinful men, though Ashtoreth and Confucius fail them, though Buddha and Brahma fail them, though Socrates and Muhammad fail them, though philosophies and prophecies fail them, though Oriental and Occidental hierarchies fail them, though angels and saints fail them, though councils and creeds and connections fail them, the name of Jesus will not fail them; for, "at its utterance walls of sin must fall, temples of superstition must crumble, juggernauts of cruelty must crash to pieces, the black horse of death and the red horse of carnage fall on their haunches."

> "I cannot see the Christ-child
> For the soldiers marching past.
> I cannot hear the angels
> For the bugle's angry blast;
> But I know the bells are ringing;
> And that faith and hope are clinging
> To the Day
> When love shall crown the world at last.
>
> "I cannot see the Christ-child
> For the smoke is in my eyes.

I cannot hear the shepherds,
For the little children's cries;
But I know the bells are ringing,
And I think I hear the singing
Of the Day
When peace like morning dawn shall rise."

—Hugh Thomson Kerr

Though there is no pardon, no peace, no purity, no salvation, no death-triumph, no heavenly inheritance incorruptible and undefiled, no element of redemption in any other names, there is one Name which cannot fail them. It is the name of Jesus of Nazareth—"The same yesterday, and to day, and for ever"—the Son whom "the Father sent . . . to be the Saviour of the world." But, whether heard or unheard, that Name is omnipotence and wisdom and love and sacrifice, at the throne of God. And to him that sits upon the throne, and constantly and graciously surveys the world, it is the accepted symbol of an atonement coextensive with sin—and also the Name which, by the purpose and power of God, is to swallow up all other names—the name above every name!

"No other Way, no other Name—
My heart is kindled to a flame,
As thus with steadfast faith I see
No other Way or Name for me.

"Loud voices cry, lo here, lo there,
Wise men are seeking everywhere
New lights that gleam o'er hills and plain
And tremble far across the main.

"Still springs my thought exultant, free—

No other Way or Name for me.
I am the Way, the Truth, the Life
Sounds clear through all surrounding strife.

"My soul no other stair can climb
To where eternal glories shine.
And so in storm or calm I see
No other Way or Name for me."

4.
Forty in the Bible

The word *forty* is a prominent word among prominent words in the Bible.
For example:

"Isaac was forty years old when . . ." (Gen. 25:20)

"Esau forty years old when . . ." (Gen. 20:34)

"Forty cows" (Gen. 32:15)

"Forty days and forty nights" (Ex. 24:18)

"Forty sockets of silver" (Ex. 25:19-21)

"Forty thousand soldiers" (see Num. 2:19)

"Forty stripes he may give him" (Deut. 25:2-3).

"Forty sons" (Judg. 12:14)

"David slew the men of seven hundred chariots . . . and forty thousand horsemen" (2 Sam. 10:18).

"Forty camels" (2 Kings 8:9)

"Forty cubits" (Ezek. 41:2)

"Forty shekels of silver" (Neh. 5:15)

Joash "reigned forty years in Jerusalem" (2 Chron. 24:1).

Let us consider a few of the events related to the word *forty* in the Bible.

The Forty of Time

Today, we think of time. Often we have heard and answered the question, "What time is it?"

So quickly our years go forever into the tomb of time—never to be RElived or UNlived. How brief are forty years! Human life at the longest on this earth is as "a vapour, that appeareth for a little time, and then vanisheth away" (Jas. 4:14).

Human life at the longest is just like the glimpse of a passing ship, a footprint on a sea-lashed shore, the stay of the postman at the door, the breath of a buffalo on a winter's morn, one lightning swift swing of the clock of time.

At the longest and happiest, life is just one burst of music down a busy street. At its longest and saddest, life is just one quick sob in the night. Death has been busy, night and day, among young and old, all the years.

Death's only flowers are faded garlands on coffin lids.

Death's only music is the sob of broken hearts.

Death's only pleasure fountains are the falling tears.

Death's only gold is the bones scattered at the grave's mouth.

Death's only palace is a huge mausoleum.

Death's only light is the darkness of the tomb.

Many eyes in which, during forty years, the light of love once gleamed are closed in the sleep of death. Voices we once loved and loved to hear have been silenced by death. Hands we once grasped or held have been folded by the enemy of us all—death. Hearts that once held others in affection for forty years are now as still as tombstones, in graveyards.

Gone forever all these forty years—every month, every week, every day, every hour, every minute, every second of all the forty. Not one year of the forty can we relive or unlive. Not one month of any year, not one week of any month, not one day of any week, not one hour of any day, not one minute of any hour, not one second of any minute—can any of us RElive or UNlive. Therefore, we should give our best to God all the time, being "doers of the Word and not hearers only."

The Forty of Rain

Think of the great flood in Noah's time. Genesis 7:17 says: "And the flood was forty days upon the earth."

Think of Noah. "There were giants in those days." Among them, Noah, like Enoch, moved with almighty God. He feared God. He helped men. He is called in the Bible "a preacher of righteousness" (2 Pet. 2:5). When God resolved to destroy the giants and giant evils of the world, he set this righteous man to building the ark.

What was the reason for the flood? The Bible answers in Genesis 6:11-12: "The earth also was corrupt before God, and the earth was filled with violence. And God looked upon the earth, and, behold, it was corrupt; for all flesh had corrupted his way upon the earth."

And God spoke to his preacher, Noah: "The end of all flesh is come before me; for the earth is filled with violence through them; and, behold, I will destroy them with the earth" (v. 13).

Then God gave Noah instructions about building the ark: "Make thee an ark of gopher wood; rooms shalt thou make in the ark, and shalt pitch it within and without with pitch. And this is the fashion which thou shalt make it of: The length of the ark shall be three hundred cubits, the breadth of it fifty cubits, and the height of it thirty cubits. A window shalt thou make to the ark, and in a cubit shalt thou finish it above; and the door of the ark shalt thou set in side thereof with lower, second, and third stories shalt thou make it" (vv. 14-16).

Noah gave strict obedience to the command of God. "Thus did Noah; according to all that God commanded him, so did he" (v. 22).

After Noah and his kin entered the ark, it was seven days before it rained.

I suppose many folks, most of them mockers, went out to see the big boat on the dry land—no water to furnish floating power.

God spoke of the seven days: "For yet seven days, and I will cause it to rain upon the earth forty days and forty nights and every living substance that I have made will I destroy from the face of the earth" (7:4).

After seven days rain came (v. 10).

It was a rain of forty days! "And the rain was upon the earth forty days and forty nights" (v. 12). "And the flood was forty days upon the earth; and the waters increased, and bare up the ark, and it was lift up above the earth" (v. 17). What destruction! "All flesh died that moved upon the earth, both of fowl, and of cattle, and of beast, and of every creeping thing that creepeth upon the earth, and every man: All in whose nostrils was the breath of life, of all that was in the dry land died. And every living substance was destroyed which was upon the face of the ground, both man, and cattle, and the creeping things, and the fowl of the heaven; and they were destroyed from the earth; and Noah only remained alive, and they that were with him in the ark" (vv. 21-23).

These truths we learn—thinking of the rain of forty days and the flood that caused all flesh to die.

The Spirit of God will not always strive with men.

God is the God of wrath, even as he is the God of love. In wrath, God hurled oceans over mountain ranges.

God is a particular God; he gave particular directions as to building the ark. And Noah gave particular obedience. He did not use pine wood instead of gopher wood. He did not build the ark 290 cubits long instead of 300 cubits, nor 40 cubits wide instead of 50, nor 25 cubits high instead of 30 cubits, nor several windows instead of one window.

The Forty of Postmortem Tributes

Think of Jacob. His life was one long struggle between two natures—one base and the other divine. As a youth, he was a cheat. Yet even as he cheated, he was struggling to be better. As he matched wits with Laban, he was serving years of tortuous toil for the girl he loved. And "they seemed unto him but a few days for the love he had for her."

After various struggles, he gave God command of his life—and he was a new man, a prince of God. Then God changed his name to Israel. He had much property and little happiness. His sons were the twelve tribes of Israel.

There is Joseph—the most faultless and fortunate man mentioned in the book of Genesis. Sold by his brothers into slavery, he was jailed in Egypt because of refusal of Potiphar's wife's request. He was let out of jail to interpret Pharaoh's dream; Pharaoh made him prime minister. A lowly Hebrew slave boy—ruling Egypt. His forgiveness of his brothers was Christlike. He was a brilliant, benevolent ruler. Success failed to spoil him. He proved that a good man cannot put himself beyond God's care.

Jacob came to his death hour. He called his sons together to tell them what would befall them in the last days. He said: "Listen, ye sons of Jacob."

"And he charged them, and said unto them, I am to be gathered unto my people: bury me with my fathers in the cave that is in the field of Ephron the Hittite. . . . There they buried Abraham and Sarah his wife; there they buried Isaac and Rebekah his wife; and there I buried Leah . . . And when Jacob had made an end of commanding his sons, he gathered up his feet into the bed, and yielded up the ghost, and was gathered unto his people" (49:29,31,33).

After Jacob died, tears were shed and kisses bestowed. "And Joseph fell upon his father's face, and wept upon him, and kissed him" (50:1).

Then Jacob's body was embalmed. "And Joseph commanded his servants the physicians to embalm his father: and the physicians embalmed Israel. And forty days were fulfilled for him: for so are fulfilled the days of those which are embalmed and the Egyptians mourned for him threescore and ten days" (vv. 2-3).

Joseph said to King Pharaoh: "My father made me swear, saying, Lo, I die; in my grave which I have digged for me in the land of Canaan, there shalt thou bury me. Now therefore let me go up, I pray thee, and bury my father and I will come again" (v. 5).

Pharaoh made answer: "Go up, and bury thy father, according as he made thee swear" (v. 6).

There was a funeral service for Jacob. "And Joseph went up to bury his father: and with him went up all the servants of Pharaoh, the elders of his house, and all the elders of the land of Egypt. And all the house of Joseph and his brethren, and of his father's house: only their little ones and their flocks, and their herds they left in the land of Goshen. And there went up with him both chariots and horsemen: and it was a very great company" (vv. 7-9).

Back home: "Joseph returned into Egypt, he, and his brethren, and all that went up with him to bury his father, after he had buried his father" (v. 14).

All this after death. Postmortem doings. Today, there is so much postmortem love and tribute. Joseph was good to his father during life. Therefore what he did after death was not mockery—as are some after-death deeds and words today.

Jacob could not feel Joseph's tears or kisses. Jacob's ears could not hear any words of lamentation. Jacob's eyes could not see the great funeral procession when "there went up with him both chariots and horsemen: and it was a very great company."

Today, after death there are many words which dead ears cannot hear; flowers which dead noses cannot smell; kisses which cold faces cannot feel; expressions of love which cannot mend broken hearts, or reach or move them.

Frank Stanton, poet superior, rebukes us for waiting until after death to do what we should have done before death.

> "Best o' fellers fur an' wide,
> Never knowed it till he died.
> Said all roun' the neighborhood
> He was nachally no good,
> Till one day he closed his eyes
> To the worl' an' to the skies,
> Last words that we heard him say:
> 'I was allus in the way;
> Jest ain't worth a tear or sigh;
> Tell 'em all Good-by, good-by!
>
> "Best o' fellers, fur an' wide,
> Never knowed it till he died.
> Till poor souls aroun' him pressed

An' laid roses on his breast;
Folks he'd helped all unbeknown;
Little children roun' the place
Cryin'—kissin' his white face;
Best o' fellers, fur and wide,
Never knowed it till he died.

"Best o' fellers . . . That's the way
We're a-doin' day by day,—
Findin' thorns in garden sweet
When the flowers air at our feet;
Allus stumblin' in the night
When the mornin's jest in sight!
Holdin' of our love until
Hearts it might have helped air still.
Best o' fellers, fur an' wide,
Never knowed it till he died."

The Forty of Moses' Stay on Mount Sinai

Exodus 24:15,17-18: "And Moses went up into the mount
and a cloud covered the mount. And the glory of the Lord
abode upon mount Sinai. And the sight of the glory of
the Lord was like devouring fire on the top of the mount
in the eyes of the children of Israel. And Moses went into
the midst of the cloud, and gat him up into the midst
of the cloud, into the mount: and Moses was in the mount
forty days and forty nights." And during those forty days
and forty nights, of those forty days Moses said: "I was
gone up into the mount to receive the tables of stone,
even the tables of covenant. . . . And the Lord delivered
unto me two tables of stone written with the finger of
God. . . . At the end of forty days and forty nights . . .
the Lord gave me the two tables of stone, even the tables
of the covenant."

And these Ten Commandments, written by the finger of God, are not the ghostly whispers of a dead age, but their authority is just as great as when their proclamation broke the age-long silence of the desert.

God still says: "Thou shalt have no other gods before me. Thou shalt not make unto thee any graven image, or any likeness of any thing that is in heaven above, or that is in the earth beneath, or that is in the water under the earth. Thou shalt not take the name of the Lord thy God in vain; for the Lord will not hold him guiltless that taketh his name in vain. Remember the sabbath day, to keep it holy. Honor thy father and thy mother: that thy days may be long upon the land which the Lord thy God giveth thee.

"Thou shalt not kill. Thou shalt not steal. Thou shalt not bear false witness against thy neighbor. Thou shall not covet."

I ask you to ask yourself if you have kept these commandments. James writes in James 2:10: "For whosoever shall keep the whole law, and yet offend in one point, he is guilty of all." What does that mean? It means that a man who breaks one commandment is guilty of breaking all because he sins against God's authority, which is equal in all commandments.

Some men say that they have kept the Seventh Commandment. But Jesus said a man can never touch a woman and yet be guilty of adultery. "Ye have heard that it was said by them of old time, Thou shalt not commit adultery: But I say unto you, That whosoever looketh on a woman to lust after her hath committed adultery with her already in his heart" (Matt. 5:27-28).

"Thou shalt not kill." Some folks say they have not committed this crime. But in the Bible we read, "He that loveth not his brother abideth in death. Whosoever hateth his brother is a murderer: and ye know that no murderer hath eternal life abiding in him" (1 John 3:14-15).

The Forty of Prayer

God's people were disgracefully disobedient to God's commandment. The people whom God brought out from their bitter bondage in Egypt were disgracefully disobedient to God's commandments and covenants. Moses told the people whom he led as being "a stiffnecked people" (Deut. 9:6). Moses said: "Remember, and forget not, how thou provokedst the Lord thy God to wrath in the wilderness: from the day that thou didst depart out of the land of Egypt, until ye came unto this place, ye have been rebellious against the Lord. Also in Horeb ye provoked the Lord to wrath, so that the Lord was angry with you to have destroyed you" (vv. 7-8).

Moses was with God on Mount Sinai forty days and forty nights—and God delivered unto him these two tables of stone written by God's own finger (vv. 9-10)—even "the tables of the covenant."

Now listen! "And the Lord said unto me, Arise, get thee down quickly from hence; for thy people which thou hast brought forth out of Egypt have corrupted themselves; they are quickly turned aside out of the way which I commanded them; they have made them a molten image. Furthermore, the Lord spake unto me, saying, I have seen this people, and, behold, it is a stiffnecked people: let me alone, that I may destroy them, and blot out their name from under heaven: and I will make of thee a nation mightier and greater than they" (vv. 12-14).

Moses came down from the mount—while the mount burned with fire—and the tables of the covenant were in

Moses' two hands.

While Moses was on the mount, the people made a molten calf and "turned aside quickly out of the way which the Lord had commanded them" (v. 16). They believed and declared that the golden calf, not God, brought them out of their bitter bondage in Egypt—that the calf had taken the yokes of slavery off their necks, that the calf had made their backs free from the whips of their taskmasters.

Notice what Moses said about his praying for the people: "And I fell down before the Lord, as at the first, forty days and forty nights: I did neither eat bread nor drink water, because of all your sins which ye sinned, in doing wickedly in the sight of the Lord to provoke him to anger. For I was afraid of the anger and hot displeasure wherewith the Lord was wroth against you to destroy you. But the Lord hearkened unto me at that time also. And the Lord was very angry with Aaron to have destroyed him: and I prayed for Aaron also the same time" (vv. 18-20).

Forty days and forty nights praying. No eating. No drinking. But praying!

It makes us ashamed when we do not pray much about men and matters. It makes us ashamed when we remember we really pray so little. It makes us consider the wisdom of those who have spoken about prayer.

ANDREW MURRAY: "In relation to his people God works only in answer to their prayer."

A. C. DIXON: "When we depend upon men, we get what men can do—and that is something. When we depend on organization, we get what organization can do—and that is something. When we depend upon education, we get what education can do—and that is something. When we depend upon money, we get what money can do—and that is something. BUT when we depend upon God, we get what God can do."

And what our churches need is what God can do. And what our homes need is what God can do. And what our individual lives need is what God can do. And what our nation needs is what God can do.

R. A. TORREY: "Nothing lies beyond the reach of prayer except that which lies beyond the reach of God."

CHARLES H. SPURGEON: "Prayer is the one remedy for all our ills. Prayer is the sword that will cut all Gordian knots. Prayer is the key that unlocks the house of sorrow and the gates of Paradise for penitent sinners."

Concerning Jesus' prayer life, we read; "And he [Jesus] withdrew himself into the wilderness, and prayed" (Luke 5:16). "And it came to pass in those days, that he went out into a mountain to pray, and continued all night in prayer to God" (6:12).

"And in the morning, rising up a great while before day, he went out, and departed into a solitary place, and there prayed" (Mark 1:35).

As those who profess to be followers of Jesus—how many times have we gotten up a great while before day to pray? How often now do we get up a great while before day to pray—to pray for our young people in danger of throwing away in carnal pleasure's market the gold of youth God has put into their keeping—to pray for the lonely old folks in nursing homes, believing that their loved ones would be glad when they die, so that expenses of nursing homes would not be anymore?

How often now do we as Christians get up a great while before day to pray for our homes, our schools, our lost neighbors, our pastors, our churches, and our nation, so much in danger of handing down our blood-bequeathed legacies reduced in quality and in quantity? I ask. Please answer!

The Forty of Provision and Protection

"The children of Israel came unto the wilderness of Sin." There was *murmuring.* There was *hunger.* They accused Moses and Aaron of bringing them out "to kill the whole assembly with hunger." "And the whole congregation of the children of Israel murmured against Moses and Aaron in the wilderness: and the children of Israel said unto them, Would to God we had died by the hand of the Lord in the land of Egypt, when we sat by the flesh pots, and when we did eat bread to the full; for ye have brought us forth into this wilderness to kill this whole assembly with hunger" (Ex. 16:2-3). God said to Moses: "I will rain bread from heaven." And he gave them manna to eat every day.

Moses said to the people: "The Lord shall give you in the evening flesh to eat, and in the morning bread to the full." And it was SO!

Meat and bread—and plenty of it! NOTE: Moses called unto all Israel!—saying: You have seen all that the Lord did before your eyes in the land of Egypt unto Pharaoh. Your eyes have seen great miracles.

NOTE: The Miracles of Provision: "And I have led you forty years in the wilderness: your clothes are not waxen old upon you, and thy shoe is not waxen old upon thy foot" (Deut. 29:5).

NOTE: The Goodness of Prohibition:

"I led you forty years . . . have ye [not] drunk wine or strong drink" (Deut. 29:5-6).

In a great sermon before he was stoned to death, Stephen spoke: "He brought them out, after that he had shewed wonders and signs in the land of Egypt, and in the Red sea, and in the wilderness forty years" (Acts 7:36). For forty years no change of clothes. For forty years no wearing out of shoes. For forty years no clinking of wine glasses. For forty years no booze to drink. For forty years—nobody guilty of drunkenness—or arrested for disorderly conduct because of drunkenness.

We know liquor never touched an individual on whom it did not leave an indelible stain. Booze never touched a home in which it did not plant the seeds of dissolution and misery. We know booze never touched a community where it did not lower the moral tone. We know booze never touched a government whose problems it did not increase. We know forever that "wine is a mocker, strong drink is raging: and whosoever is deceived thereby is not wise."

SHAKESPEARE: "O thou invisible spirit of wine if thou hast no name to be known by, let us call thee Devil."

LINCOLN: "Liquor might have defenders, but no defense."

GLADSTONE: "The ravages of drink are greater than those of war, pestilence, and famine combined."

SIR WILFRED GRENFELL: "Alcohol has wrecked more lives, starved more children, and murdered more women than any other single factor."

We need to have the attitude toward booze that Billy Sunday had, who said: "I'll kick liquor till my toes come off. I'll claw liquor till my fingers leave my hands. I'll bite liquor till my teeth come out—and then I'll gum it to the jaws of hell."

What good has liquor ever done? What man has it made more prosperous? What home has it ever made happier? What girl has it ever made purer? What father has it ever helped in any way to make his family happier? What has broken man's scepter and torn his crown from his brow?

Liquor has so degraded man that he is below the brute and the hog in the pen.

You tell me how much you drink—and I will tell you approximately how long you will live. So to be even a moderate drinker you can cut many years off your life.

Be wise—touch not! Drink not! "Woe unto him that giveth his neighbour drink, that puttest thy bottle to him, and makest him drunken also, that thou mayest look on their nakedness!" (Hab. 2:15). Yet, with all God did for them, they "erred in their hearts" and did not know God's ways. "But with whom was he grieved forty years? was it not with them that had sinned, whose carcases fell in the wilderness?" (Heb. 3:17).

Oh! I think of our nation for which God has done so many wonderful things! I wonder if he has not been long grieved with us when he considers our wickedness—our disgraceful booze bill, our dishonorable crime rate?

The late J. Edgar Hoover of the Federal Bureau of Investigation wrote: "While the nation has grown only 9% since 1960, the volume of crime rose 60% in the same period of time."

How good God was to Israel! "The God of this people of Israel chose our fathers, and exalted the people when they dwelt as strangers in the land of Egypt, and with an high arm brought he them out of it. And about the time of forty years suffered he their manners in the wilderness" (Acts 13:17-18).

The Forty of Temptation

I speak of Jesus who was in all points "tempted like as we are, yet was without sin" (Heb. 4:15). "And Jesus being full of the Holy Ghost, returned from Jordan, and was led by the Spirit into the wilderness, being forty days tempted of the devil. And in those days he did eat nothing: and when they were ended, he afterward hungered" (Luke 4:1-2). "Then was Jesus led up of the spirit into the wilderness to be tempted of the devil" (Matt. 4:1).

There he fasted forty days and forty nights (Matt. 4:2).

After Jesus was baptized, "Immediately the Spirit driveth him into the wilderness" (Mark 1:12).

"And he was there in the wilderness forty days tempted of Satan; and was with the wild beasts; and the angels ministered unto him" (v. 13). "Being forty days tempted," Luke says.

Let us consider the three temptations after the forty days among the wild beasts in the wilderness. After the fast of forty days and forty nights, Jesus was hungry. "And when the tempter came to him, he said, If thou be the Son of God, command that these stones be made bread" (Matt. 4:3).

In the *first temptation*, Satan was saying: "Serve thyself."

Note the *second temptation*. "Then the devil taketh him up into the holy city, and setteth him on a pinnacle of the temple, and said unto him, If thou be the Son of God, cast thyself down: for it is written, He shall give his angels charge concerning thee: and in their hands they shall bear thee up, lest at any time thou dash thy foot against a stone" (vv. 5-6). Satan was really saying: "Let God serve you."

Note the *third temptation:* "Again, the devil taketh him up into an exceeding high mountain, and sheweth him all the kingdoms of the world, and the glory of them; and saith unto him, All things will I give thee, if thou wilt fall down and worship me" (vv. 8-9). The devil was saying: "Let me serve you."

The temptations teach that it was a real assault, a real Satan, a real Christ, a real temptation, a real victory for

Christ, a real defeat for Satan. The temptation of forty days in the wilderness where he was among wild beasts and where angels ministered unto him was not a vision, not a mere legend, not a parabolic narrative, not a panoramic imagination, but a real experience with a real devil which Christ suffered.

The Forty of Resurrection Revelation

After Jesus rose from the grave—the dead—he gave commandments unto the apostles whom he had chosen (Acts 1:2). To the apostles he showed himself alive; "being seen of them forty days, and speaking of the things pertaining to the kingdom of God" (Acts 1:3).

He showed himself alive by many undeniable proofs after his PASSION—his death on Calvary's cross where he was made a curse for us. "I am he that liveth, and was dead; and, behold, I am alive for evermore. Amen." Jesus, born in denial of the laws of life, was raised from the dead in defiance of the laws of death—our living Christ.

A living Christ—no pale Christ of historical imagination.

A living Christ—no mere dream Christ of culture and romance.

Our contemporary Christ—no mere heroic Christ of the poet's song; no fading artistic Christ of the painter's brush; no cold marble Christ of the sculptor's chisel; no ivory Christ on a crucifix, giving an expression of the worship of defeat.

A living Christ—no mere eulogized Christ of the orator's rhetoric; no radiant apparition Christ of yesterday; no vanished Christ canonized by the historian's pen; no coffined Christ of the embalmer's art. No Christ remote. No Christ inaccessible. But a Christ alive! Alive—to the end of unending eternity—acknowledging no mastery in hostile

circumstances. Alive, offering the inexhaustible fountains
of his strength. Alive, keeping pace with the most unex-
pected challenges. Alive—able, willing, mighty to help—our
eternal contemporary. Alive, making the impenetrable
walls of life and death magnificent apertures. Alive,
changing bleak limitation into immeasurable expanse.

Woefully inadequate all words fully to portray Jesus—as
he IS and will forever be in his glory, his goodness, his
grace, his greatness! Let speak forty orators from whose
mouths words come like flights of golden arrows. Let write
forty writers from whose pens words drop like golden
pollen from the stems of shaken lilies. Let play all musicians and forty orchestras who have the genius to build
rhythmic palaces of music before the eyes of our souls.
Let paint forty painters whose brushes put on canvas all
the glories of sunsets, sunrises, and starry heavens. Let
sing forty choirs whose anthems are eternity and glory.

A woeful inadequacy will possess and oppress all as
all these try to set forth Jesus—Son of man without sin,
Son of God with power. No—not if all modes of expression
and portrayal were active for forty times forty years.

89

5.
Destruction of Sin

Uses of the Word Destruction

Ahaziah was son of Jehoram, king of Judah. Jehoram was thirty-two years old when he began his reign—and he reigned in Jerusalem eight years—"and departed without being desired."

"And the inhabitants of Jerusalem made Ahaziah, his youngest son, king in his stead."

"He also walked in the ways of the house of Ahab: for his mother was his counsellor to do wickedly. Wherefore he did evil in the sight of the Lord like the house of Ahab: for they were his counsellors after the death of his father to his destruction" (2 Chron. 22:3-4).

We read of "[Uzziah, king of Judah,] when he was strong, his heart was lifted up to his destruction" (2 Chron. 26:16).

Esther, pleading with King Ahasuerus, for her Jewish people, said: "For how can I endure to see the evil that shall come unto my people? or how can I endure to see the destruction of my kindred?" (Esther 8:6).

Eliphaz, the Temanite, said to Job:

"Thou shalt be hid from the scourge of the tongue: neither shalt thou be afraid of destruction when it cometh. At destruction and famine thou shalt laugh: neither shall thou be afraid of the beasts of the earth" (Job 5:21-22).

Job, asking questions through lips festering with disease, said of God; "Hell is naked before him, and destruction has no covering" (Job 26:6). He asked: "Is not destruction to the wicked?" (31:3).

David, speaking of his enemies perishing in the presence of the Lord, said: "Destructions are come to a perpetual end" (Ps. 9:6). And: "Thou castedst them down into destruction" (73:18). And: "Thou turnest man to destruction" (90:3).

And these comforting words spoke King David:

"Thou shalt not be afraid for the terror by night; nor for the arrow that flieth by day; Nor for the pestilence that walketh in darkness; nor for the destruction that wasteth at noonday" (91:5-6).

And David also spoke of God "who redeemeth thy life from destruction" (103:4).

Solomon spoke of God laughing at man's calamity—when man "set at nought all of God's counsel"—saying: "I will mock . . . when your fear cometh as desolation, and your destruction cometh as a whirlwind" (Prov. 1:26-27).

And Solomon said: "Pride goeth before destruction" (16:18). "The fool's mouth is his destruction" (18:7). "Hell and destruction are never full" (27:20). He also spoke of those who are "appointed to destruction" (31:8).

Isaiah the Old Testament evangelist spoke of "the besom of destruction" (14:23); "the city of destruction" (19:18); and "wasting and destruction" (59:7).

He also spoke of the blessed time when: "Violence shall no more be heard in thy land, wasting nor destruction within thy borders; but thou shalt call thy walls Salvation, and thy gates Praise" (60:18).

Jeremiah, the weeping prophet, said: "Heal me, O Lord, and I shall be healed; save me, and I shall be saved; for thou art my praise" (17:14). "Let them be confounded that persecute me, but let not me be confounded: let them be dismayed, but let not me be dismayed: bring upon them the day of evil, and destroy them with double destruction" (v. 18).

Jeremiah also said: "The sound of battle is in the land, and of great destruction" (50:22).

The prophet Hosea spoke of how God had said he would do certain things for the people—in these words: "I will ransom thee from the power of the grave; I will redeem thee from death: O, death, I will be thy plague. O, grave, I will be thy destruction" (Hos. 13:14).

And Jesus, Teacher above all teachers, as a great palm tree in a desert of mediocrity, said: "Broad is the way, that leadeth to destruction" (Matt. 7:13).

Paul, writing to the Romans, said: "Destruction and misery are in their ways" (Rom. 3:16). And: "God, willing to shew his wrath, and to make his power known, endured with much longsuffering the vessels of wrath fitted to destruction" (Rom. 9:22).

Paul, writing to the Philippians, spoke of who "are the enemies of the Cross of Christ: whose end is destruction" (Phil. 3:18-19).

Paul also used the word *destruction* when he wrote of:

The "sudden destruction" (1 Thess. 5:3). "Punished with everlasting destruction" (2 Thess. 1:9). "Lusts, which drown men in destruction" (1 Tim. 6:9).

And the apostle Peter spoke of those "who . . . bring upon themselves swift destruction" (2 Pet. 2:1).

When we think of the destruction here mentioned we should recall Job's answer: "His eyes shall see his destruction, and he shall drink of the wrath of the Almighty" (Job 21:20). And: "For destruction from God was a terror to me, and by reason of his highness I could not endure" (Job 31:23). And Proverbs 10:29, "The way of the Lord is strength to the upright; but destruction shall be to the workers of iniquity." And "destruction shall be to the workers of iniquity" (Prov. 21:15).

All these verses speak to us of the

Destruction of Sin

There are ten words that define the awfulness of sin and the destruction thereof.

G. Campbell Morgan says: Sin is unlikeness of God. Wrong done to God. Distance from God.

But in the Bible, there are ten Greek words that define *sin* in ten different aspects.

1. *Hamartia*—missing the mark. Act—and the result of the action. "Wherefore, as by one man sin entered into the world, and death by sin; and so death passed upon all men, for that all have sinned" (Rom. 5:12).

2. *Hamartama*—disobedience to a divine law.

3. *Asebeia*—ungodliness, irreligious, opposition to God. "For the wrath of God is revealed from heaven against all ungodliness and unrighteousness of men, who hold the truth in unrighteousness" (Rom. 1:18).

4. *Parakoa*—failing to hear when God speaks, careless-

ness, inattention, disobedience, failure to obey when God speaks. Romans 5:18: "Therefore as by the offence of one judgment came upon all men to condemnation; even so by the righteousness of one the free gift came upon all men unto justification of life"

5. *Anomia*—contempt for law, contrary to law, iniquity. "Then said I, Woe is me! for I am undone; because I am a man of unclean lips, and I dwell in the midst of a people of unclean lips: for mine eyes have seen the King, the Lord of hosts" (Isa. 6:5). "Even so ye also outwardly appear righteous unto men, but within ye are full of hypocrisy and iniquity" (Matt. 23:28).

6. *Paranomia*—wickedness. Peter, speaking of the marks of the false teachers who are like Balaam, wrote: "Which have forsaken the right way, and are gone astray, following the way of Balaam the son of Bosor, who loved the wages of unrighteousness; but was rebuked for his iniquity: the dumb ass speaking with man's voice forbad the madness of the prophet" (2 Pet. 2:15-16).

7. *Parabasis*—breaking a distinctively recognized commandment. "Thou that makest thy boast of the law, through breaking the law dishonourest thou God?" (Rom. 2:23).

8. *Paraptoma*—a wilful sin, a mistake, a fault. "I marvel that ye are so soon removed from him that called you into the grace of Christ unto another gospel: which is not another: but there be some that trouble you, and would pervert the gospel of Christ" (Gal. 1:6-7)

9. *Agnoama*—error, sin, resulting from ignorance. "But into the second went the high priest alone once every year, not without blood, which he offered for himself, and for the errors of the people" (Heb. 9:7).

10. *Hetama*—failure in duty, failure to render full mea-

sure. Diminution, inferiority. "Now if the fall of them be the riches of the world, and the diminishing of them the riches of the Gentiles; how much more their fulness?" (Rom. 11:12).

Paul in Romans 1—2 gives us a history of the nature and the fruit of sin. That sums up in "being filled with all unrighteousness"—a picture of a full cup of characteristics that reveal how unlike God man is, and how far he is from God and how wrong man has been in his treatment of God.

We need a true concept of sin. We need to see sin through God's eyes—yes, through the crimson lenses of the cross.

We must think of sin as the

Curse of All Curses

Back behind all human ages, the words *SIN* and *SINS* take us beyond all time—into awful, infinite depths. Back to the most terrible fact of God's universe—the fact of sin, life's most dreadful and inexorable curse.

Sin, so like a river, beginning in a quiet spring, ending in a tumultuous sea.

Sin—the desert breath that drinks up every dew.

Sin—the death head set amidst life's feast.

Sin—the power that reversed man's nature, destroyed the harmony of his powers, threw him, woefully deranged, miserable, ungoverned, erratic, lost, into interminable leagues of night.

Sin—the evil that subverted the constitutional order of his nature, dismantled him of his nobility, brought him in unconditional surrender to diabolical power, caused him treacherously to give up the keys of the soul's citadel placed in his keeping.

Abroad in this world today are many false conceptions of sin. The literary and aesthetic conception of sin, which says that sin is a "disagreeable hindrance to the smooth ongoing of the social machinery." The scientific conception, which says that sin is "an upward stumble in man's progress." The Ingersollic conception, which says that sin is a "nightmare caused by too much appetite and too little digestion!" The philosophic conception which says, "Sin is youthful indiscretion, egotistic abnormality, perverted taste."

False, false as the teaching of Satan, all these conceptions.

False all conceptions whereby sin is labeled psychological hysteria, psychic rebellion, error, flaw, immaturity.

No language lending respectability to sin, improves sin.

W. B. Riley said: "The preaching, the teaching, the theology that does not make sin STINK is puny preaching, trite teaching, and tragic theology."

John Henry Jowett said: "I covet no language that lends respectability to sin. You can do a man no sorer injury than to lighten his conception of the awfulness of SIN."

Cardinal Newman: "You cannot make sin respectable by dressing it in fine clothes."

You cannot improve smallpox by putting the patient in an art gallery. You cannot make a pigsty any less a pigsty by planting flowers around it. The dead pollution of leprosy is not lessened by clothing its victims in purple and fine linen.

Sin, the aggregation of all evils, the quintessence of all horrors, entered the world. And death, the sum of all penalties, by sin (Rom. 5:12).

Jesus, who found remedies for hunger, disease, madness, and physical death, who, by a word, hushed storms, was "amazed and sore troubled" by sin's dread power. Its weight fell upon him in soul agony and bloody sweat. From its vast abyss his feet, the feet of Deity, drew back with trembling as he faced the time when he wrought for man deliverance from sin's ruin, when he was made a curse because of sin's curse (Gal. 3:13).

Ghastly great among life's factors, awful, universal, inescapable—the fact of sin.

And if sin becomes an unaffrighting and undisturbing commonplace that never startles us into pain, our preaching, our teaching, our Christian activities become playthings.

Behind all our phraseology, we must retain the tremendous sense of the ruin of sin, coveting no phraseology that lends it respectability, knowing that we deal, not with trifles and puny pettiness, but with blinding, appalling enormities!

Whatever ignores sin, whether literature, government, drama, religion, preaching, teaching, inevitably fails to declare God's truth—fails to compass the necessities of mankind. To this shameful failure much modern writing, much modern teaching, much modern preaching is doomed. We cannot drown the stench of sin's carrion under floodtides of philosophical perfume.

Sin, a fatal mischief of the heart, a seed big with future pain and grief, the quintessence of all horrors, the causative element of all world suffering, is no whirlwind creating a slight disturbance, but a hot sirocco blasting all gardens.

No light discord—a thunderbolt that shatters the organ into splinters, leaving it without shape or tone.

No pen knife—a guillotine.

No slight jerk of the hiccoughs—the agonies of sciatica.

No lame Mephibosheth—a diabolical Jezebel.

No crude catapult—a bursting bomb.

No quiet pool—a maelstrom.

No cool rill—a perpetual lava rush scorching its way through green fields.

Stern fact that magical science, with all its marvelous accomplishments, cannot get rid of—SIN! For science can nowhere find a sea deep enough to drown remorse or that contains water enough to wash away sin's pollution.

Awful fact that education cannot teach away—sin!

Dread disease that all medical skill cannot cure—sin!

Dark demonic vulture that all our modes of progress cannot outtravel—sin!

Sin is folly, devastation, disorder, death—a madness in the brain, a poison in the heart, an opiate in the will, a frenzy in the imagination, a darkness that invests man's whole moral being!

The intolerable burden of a soul destined to exist forever.

The moth and rust that consume the mind.

The sum of all cruelty, all terror, all wrong, all horror.

When a man sins he falls, he is not on his way to something better. He is on his way to something worse. He is on his way to destruction.

Sin—manifest inwardly in discrowned faculties, in unworthy love, in sordid satisfactions, in brutalized spirits—is the curse of all curses—blighting earth's flowery vales with crime, darkening earth's seas with wrath, grouping earth's isles as lairs of lust, making many places in our cities deserts of hell. It is in all climes, in all times, a ruin, wretched ruin.

Sin is a Goliath of power.

Sin is a wild Absalom of rebellion.

Sin is a sullen Macbeth of villainy.

Sin is a greedy Midas of avarice.

Sin is an audaciously loathsome Judas of treachery.

Sin is a thieving Sapphira of falsehood.

Sin is a cruel Ahab of covetousness.

Sin is a destructive Cleopatra of lust.

Sin is a bold Belshazzar of irreverence.

Sin is a bloody Jael of slaughter.

Sin is a merciless Nero of evil.

Sin is an intolerably haughty Nebuchadnezzar of pride.

Sin is a painted Jezebel of murder.

Sin is an ambitious Athaliah of usurpation.

And all these in one.

Ten thousand times ten thousand homes it has broken.

Many nations it has cast upon the tragic ruins of history.

It is more vicious than the teeth of the piranha. It is a bloodhound of perdition that never loses a trail.

Let us never forget that

Christ Is the Cure for All that Sin Causes

Christ will cause the desert sin has made to blossom as the rose.

Christ can build again the walls and gates that sin has broken down.

Christ can unite again the homes that sin has broken.

Christ can rebuild the home that the hurricane of sin has swept away. He can!

Christ can make the liar truthful. He can!

Christ can make the thief honest. He can!

Christ can make the drunkard sober. He can!

Christ can restore that which sin has taken away. He can!

Christ can restore the years the locusts have eaten. He can!

Christ—the great Emancipator!

"For the law of the Spirit of life in Christ Jesus hath made me free from the law of sin and death" (Rom. 8:2).

Christ Jesus only is the everlasting source of human salvation. He only, by a work consistent with the character of God, can break the power which holds us in chains, avert punishment which threatens us, fortify with fresh sanctions the law which we have broken, and, reconciling justice with mercy, open to mankind the fountains of grace. Through him the law is vindicated, the holiness of God doubly honored and mercy in richest munificence proclaimed to the sinner.

Sin is debt; divine forgiveness is God's acceptance of the crimson coin of Christ's blood as payment for the debt.

Sin is a stain; divine forgiveness is the bath which cleans it away.

Sin is dross; divine forgiveness is the furnace which burns it out.

Sin is darkness; divine forgiveness is the light which dispels it. Sin is a burden; divine forgiveness is the burial of it in the sea's depths.

Sin is a poison; divine forgiveness is the antidote that eliminates it.

Sin is a coral reef on which ships go down; divine forgiveness is the power that removes it.

Sin is the soul miasma; divine forgiveness is the pure wind that sweeps it away.

Sin is a sewer pipe; divine forgiveness is the transformation that makes it a luxuriant garden.

Sin is the blotted and blurred record; divine forgiveness is the erasure of the sinful pages from life's book.

So—Don't forget that:

Without Jesus—in death there is no assurance; without

Jesus—in trouble there is no refuge; without Jesus—in temptation there is no strength; without Jesus—in disease there is no courage; without Jesus—in clamor there is no judgment; without Jesus—in sin there is no grace; without Jesus—in perplexity there is no prompting; without Jesus— in darkness there is no light; without Jesus—in storms there is no calm.

But with Jesus through faith in his Name, trusting in the omnipotence of his blood, you have assurance of victory over sin and the world and eternal punishment. By fastening your faith to Christ's great sacrifice and nothing else, that sacrifice shall evermore speak for you. And one day, because of this, you shall find yourself standing before God unashamed and unafraid, faultless and free from every stain—a sinner washed in the blood of the Lamb.

6.
Recognition in Heaven

"I shall go to him" (2 Sam. 12:23).
"Then shall I know even as also I am known"
(1 Cor. 13:12).

I do not claim that all the thoughts I shall present here
are mine only. I do not say that all these words were born
in my heart alone. I do not declare that any light I may
kindle comes from altars where only my mental and medi-
tative coals burn. But you may rest assured that every word
is written with the prayer to bless and not blast, to help
and not hurt, as I write from a heart that would do you
good and not evil all the days of my life—as I write about
a subject concerning which there should never be any
doubt in any believer's heart.

Of all the questions that have exercised and still exercise
the mind of man, none are more interesting and important
than those that relate to man's origin and destiny. The
whence and *whither* of personal life are both fundamental
questions. Both, too, are bound up with religion. From
time immemorial, man has looked into the years, backward
and forward, reminiscently and prophetically, wondering,
wondering! In those far-back, primitive days when life

seemed simple, something in man revolted from the thought that life could end in endless sleep. And, even now, in this our day, when we have let go of some of the sweet simplicities of the old-time religion, we are apt to think of the future life as less obvious, less real, more ghostly, more metaphorical. Thus we become the victims of time and space.

John Henry Jowett said: "We must preach on these great subjects whose vastness almost terrifies us as we approach them." And I am frank to say that the subject of heavenly recognition is a subject whose vastness almost terrifies me as I approach it; but its solemn splendor thrills my soul—and its truth warms my heart.

There come times to us all when we wish Christ had said more. There are great questions which we should like to have put to him, and on which we should like to have received exact and definite information. So it is with this question of heavenly recognition which presents to us a problem of unusual interest. The question comes to us distinctly amid the roar of the complex machinery of our modern life. It presses down upon our hearts when the cares of life press heavily on our shoulders. The question comes to us when we would be materialistic; but the spiritual will not stay down; the oft-smothered but unquenchable fires of the spiritual burn—and we find ourselves in times of unspeakable loneliness, in periods of meditation, in times when the heart is crushed with some great sorrow, asking: Shall we know each other in heaven?

Well, let me say with Thurlow Weed, noted American journalist: "I cannot believe that the purpose of our creation is fulfilled by our short existence here. To me the existence of another world, where we know others and others know us, is a necessary supplement of this, to adjust its inequalities and imbue it with moral significance."

Now it is one thing to avoid reckless assertion without any foundation. It is undoubtedly another thing to have so little trust in God that we are afraid to make a fair inference concerning the life beyond such as we would unhesitatingly make in like conditions here. I believe in recognition in heaven as surely as I believe there is a God. If consciousness, character, love, memory, and fellowship are in that life, why should there be any question about it? May God help me for your sakes to take the doctrine of "heavenly recognition" out of the region of surmise and speculation into the region of absolute certainty.

Let us consider heavenly recognition from what implications of its rejection implies. Its rejection implies:

The Utter Forgetfulness of Our Earth Life and Friends

In other words, the blotting out of the faculty of memory. Shall we forget forever those whom we knew on earth? Shall we forever be unfamiliar with those with whom we walked and talked in the sacred intimacies of life on earth? Shall we in the glory come near to those with whom we locked arms in sweet comradeship and joined hands in holy endeavor and with whom we ran in lockstep toward noble goals on earth and, up there, know them not? Was Thomas H. Bayly lying when he said: "Friends depart, and memory takes them to her caverns, pure and deep"? Will death come like some grim husbandman who prunes a vine and cuts away from the vine of our being the branch of memory?

If we shall not know one another, why then this undying memory of departed ones, this aching void that is never filled on earth? Alas for us! Then we are worse off than the lower animals. The calf is taken from the cow; the

cow mourns for a night—and then in a day her calf is
forgotten. The kittens are taken from the mother; and after
a day or so of restless wandering the mother forgets the
kittens. The dove mourns for a day in the elms over the
nest wrecked by the storm and for the birdies drowned
by the flood—and then the birdies are remembered no
more. But the poor human mother never forgets as long
as she has her faculties. When her head is white with
the snow of many years and her feet all faltering go down
the sunset trail, you can bring tears into her eyes by men-
tioning the child that died in her arms forty years before.
And when the old father passes the eightieth milestone
of life, a useless cumberer on the earth, he will weep at
the mere mention of the wild boy that broke his father's
heart and despised his father's counsel. Through the shad-
owy past, like a tomb searcher, memory runs thus, lifting
each shroud that time cast over buried hopes.

Rejection of This Doctrine Defeats the Expectancy of the World

Even among those reared at pagan firesides and taught
by pagan teachers, there is the yearning for other-world
recognition. The great pagan teachers believed and taught
that the fires of life, when they died down, would not
leave cold ashes. Ultimately this does not prove anything.
But it does suggest this: deep down in human intuition
and deep down in the human soul God Almighty has not
left man without a witness. As one has said: "The profound
cry of the human soul and the thought of human consciousness is the fact of heavenly recognition." In all lands
and in all ages the theory of recognition in the future world
is received. What form of religion planted this thing which
Christianity confirms? No form of religion, for it is received

under all forms of religion. It is a sentiment universally implanted; it is a feeling universally vital; it is an anticipation universally dynamic; it is an instinct universal. Is it God-implanted? Then it is rightfully implanted.

Cicero who lived before Christ's day said: "Oh, glorious day when I shall retire from this low and sordid scene to associate with the divine assemblage of departed spirits . . . with my dear Cato, the best of sons and the most faithful of men. It was my sad fate to lay his body on the funeral pile. If I seemed to bear his death with fortitude, it was by no means because I did not feel sensibly the loss I had sustained. It was because I was supported by the consoling reflection that we should not be long separated."

Homer, great man to the Greeks, tells of Ulysses' meeting his mother in the spirit world and recognizing her. Virgil represents Aeneas as meeting with his friends over there and talking with them. Old Socrates was nerved to drink the hemlock because of the thought of meeting the friends who had gone before.

These are just a few glimpses through the eye of a needle at the landscape of pagan teachers—but a taste of their philosophy, but a drink at the spring of their poetry.

But, in the lower order of beings is not the same desire—clothed more raggedly, of course, but as strong nevertheless—vital? Longfellow said that:

"Even in savage bosoms
    There are longings, yearnings, strivings
    For the good they comprehend not;
    There are feeble hands and helpless,
    Groping blindly in the darkness,
    Touch God's right hand in the darkness."

An ancient heathen king would whisper a message into the ear of the servant and then cut his servant's head off to send the message to the other side. Among the Danes, when a master died, the servant would sometimes slay himself that he might serve his master in the future world.

The Indian warrior died, and his wife and others of his followers were slain that they might follow him to the happy hunting ground. The Indian's bows and arrows were buried with him that he might have weapons in the other world. And his dog was slain and buried with him that the dog might, in the happy hunting ground, run the deer without weariness.

Repulsive, indeed, these incidents and practices to our cultured minds. Yet, robbed of their objectionable features, they cause us to believe that deep down in the human soul, even among the most heathen of peoples and among the religions of pagan peoples, there is something that rests not and is not still in its longing for fellowship. That proclaims the reality of recognition in the future state. The German believes it. The Arab believes it. The Chinaman, eating rats in Hong Kong, believes it. The Eskimo, feasting on blubber amid the ice floes of the north, believes it. The Bushman of Africa, with the mentality that can count but two, believes it. The Turk believes it. The cultured college professor, who has not gotten away from his mother's religion, believes it. Under every sky, by every river, in every zone, this belief is held. And, as T. Dewitt Talmage says, a principle universally implanted must be God-implanted, and if God-implanted it must be a lawful expectation.

> "Oh, ye weary, sad and tossed,
>   Droop not, faint not, by the way;
> Ye shall find the loved and just

> In that land of perfect day.
> Harp strings touched by angel hands
> Murmured in my raptured ear;
> Evermore the sweet truth stands,
> 'We shall know each other there.' "

Remember that

Heaven Is a Place, but It Is Not a Place of Contraction

It is a place of enlarged knowledge, a place where I shall know more than I know here, a place where I know others better than I know them here, a place where they shall know me better than they do here. "For we know in part, and we prophesy in part. But when that which is perfect is come, then that which is in part shall be done away" (1 Cor. 13:9-10).

Conceptions of heaven vary. Robert Hall said his chief conception of heaven was—rest; Wilberforce—love; Southey—place of intellectual activity and enjoyment; Foster—unfolding of all the mysteries of truth and providence; Leighton—world of perfect spirituality and holiness; Payson—"Where I shall be with Christ and serve him and enjoy him forever."

But unite all the conceptions and add to them all that heart can wish or mind conceive, and you will see that in them all and through them all is the thought that cannot be hidden of enlarged knowledge—expansion, not contraction.

John Evans, the great Scottish minister, was seated in his study. His wife came in and said, "My dear, do you think we will know each other in heaven?" He turned to her and said: "My dear, do you think we will be bigger fools in heaven than we are here?" Now that is not a flippant answer; no, not at all. The idea that we shall not know one another in heaven makes it appear that we shall know less in heaven than we do here.

But there our knowledge will be increased and enlarged above our knowledge here as the oak is enlarged above the acorn, as the butterfly is enlarged above the chrysalis, as an ode of Milton is enlarged above the letter Z, as a steel girder above the sinew and bone of a man's arm, as the gleam of a star over the glow of a glowworm. As the steel leviathans of today surpass the old bateau, as the incandescent light transcends the tallow dip, as the macadam road excels the turtle path, as the thinking of a philosopher goes higher and deeper than the thinking of a child, as Niagara goes beyond the mud puddle in glory, as the Alps possess more majesty than the prairie dog's burrow—so will that which is heavenly outshine and outgrow and outreach that which is earthly.

"We shall know each other better
When the mists have rolled away."

The higher law always sets aside the lower. Vegetable law sets aside mineral law—and there is growth. Animal law sets aside vegetable law—and there is nutrition. Mental law transcends the physical law—and the blood is consumed by thought and emotion. The law of life, outbreaking life, transcends the law of death. So the heavenly transcends the earthly—and as God's thoughts are high above our thoughts now, so our thinking in heaven and our knowing in heaven will transcend our thinking here and excel our knowing here.

Job said: "My purposes are broken off" (17:11). But he did not say, "All my purposes will be broken off!" Browning said: "On earth the broken arcs, in heaven the perfect round."

In heaven we shall be consciously alive, in a life richer, larger, fuller. We shall be personally alive, under conditions which impose no limitations upon us. We shall be outside the fettering limitations of time and space.

Dr. Alexander Maclaren said: "Every man that has died is at this instant in full possession of all his faculties, in the intensest exercise of his capacities, standing somewhere in God's presence, and feeling in every fiber of his being. That life which comes after death is not less real, not less great but more great, not less intense and full, but more intense and full than the mingled life which, lived here on earth, was a center of life surrounded with a crust and circumference of mortality."

> "Not now, but in the coming years
>   It may be in the better land;
> We'll read the meaning of our tears,
>   And there, sometime, we'll understand.

> "We'll catch the broken thread again,
>   And finish what we here began;
> Heav'n will the mysteries explain,
>   And then, ah, then, we'll understand."

> —MAXWELL N. CORNELIUS

Do you remember how God described himself in a passage which Jesus used as an argument for the reality of the life beyond? He said: "I *am* the God of Abraham, Isaac, and Jacob!" Not I *was* the God of Abraham when he was alive; not I *was* the God of Isaac when he was on earth; not I *was* the God of Jacob when he lived on earth! But the relation was an actual and existing one. God stood to them in the relation of their personal God—who knew them as Abraham, Isaac, and Jacob! Thank God for that!

God counts the hairs of our heads. God numbers our footsteps. Not a sparrow falls but he knows. The Good Shepherd knows his sheep by name. Our names are written in heaven. Jesus said: "Rejoice, because your names are written in heaven" (Luke 10:20).

Recognition in Heaven a Fact

Up there we shall not be lost and merged into some vast ocean of being. We shall exist and live as ourselves. Life hereafter will be conscious, individual, personal.

When we reach there after our long journey, it will not be as the Amazon losing itself in the Atlantic or as the Mississippi losing its identity in the Gulf of Mexico.

> "The stars shine over the earth,
> The stars shine over the sea,
> The stars look up to the mighty God,
> The stars look down on me.
> The stars shall live for a million years,
> A million years and a day,
> But Christ and I will live and love
> When the stars have passed away."

Now consider some Bible assertions as to heavenly recognition.

Jesus to unbelieving Jews.—Jesus said to the unbelieving Jews that they would in the future world see Abraham, Isaac, and Jacob while they themselves would be thrust out. Thus to my mind does the Bible speak of heaven as a great family circle. Some day they shall come from the north and the south and the east and the west and take their places at the marriage supper of Moses and the Lamb. Well, now, that would be a strange home circle where the members did not know each other. The Bible describes death as a sleep. If we know each other before we go to sleep, shall we not know each other when we awake? Robert Browning put a flower into the cold hand of his dead sweetheart and said: "You will wake, and remember, and understand." And I believe she will; and I know others will and waking understand and know. John Fiske said, "I believe in the immortality of the soul as a sublime fact of faith in the reasonableness of God's work." I believe in the recognition of loved ones on the other side as a mere, simple act of faith in the reasonableness of God's love. And while those unbelieving Jews would—themselves thrust out, the door shut nevermore to open, in the world of the lost—recognize Abraham and Isaac and Jacob before the throne, shall not we, standing in glory, know our best friend, our dearest loved one, from the man who died in a Mexican barroom last night? Not to do so is unthinkable.

The Bible, by many assertions, assures Christians of recognition in heaven. The Christian religion assures us, too.

What about this Christian religion? "The crystal cannot equal it." Beautiful it is in the hope it kindles, beautiful in the sentiment it implants, beautiful in the proposition to garland and enthrone an immortal spirit.

Talmage once said something like this. I would repeat it in substance to you. Solomon says this religion is a lily. Paul says it is a crown. The Apocalypse says it is a fountain kissed with the sun. Ezekiel says it is a foliaged cedar. Christ says it is a bridegroom come to carry home a bride.

Do you agree with Solomon that it is a lily? Then pluck it and wear it over your heart. Do you say with Paul that it is a crown? Then let this be your coronation hour. Do you agree with the Apocalypse that it is a fountain kissed with the sun? Then come and slake the thirst of your soul.

Do you believe with Ezekiel that it is a foliaged cedar? Then come under its shadow. Do you say with Christ that it is a bridegroom come to carry home a bride? Then yield in full surrender to your King while God pronounces you everlastingly one.

Millions of people in the world are choosing between salvation and destruction, between light and darkness, between heaven and hell, between life and death. You will know your Savior over there. You will know your loved ones there. Then choose. Choose God. Choose God now.

Do you love the beautiful? Then go look on the Rose of Sharon, even Jesus. Do you love music? Then go there and listen to the music of his voice. Are you a mathematician? Then go and help count the years of his reign. Do you know explorers? Then urge them to join the happy throng that there they may discover the breadth of his love. Have you had the military spirit sanctified for the cause of liberty? Then get thee along the journey that there you may see the Captain of your salvation. Are you an astronomer or do you love astronomy? Then go look at the Morning Star. Are you a lawyer? Then hasten thy preparation that you may be ready to stand unashamed before him who is the judge of the quick and the dead. Are you a physician? Then, as you go on your blessed ministry of serving the sick, make ready to look on him who was wounded for our transgressions, who died, the just for the unjust, that he might bring us to God, with whose stripes we are healed.

7.
The Perfect City

"Abraham . . . looked for a city which hath foundations, whose builder and maker is God" (Heb. 11:8,10).

"Now they desire a better country, that is, an heavenly: wherefore God is not ashamed to be called their God: for he hath prepared for them a city" (Heb. 11:16).

"Ye are come unto Mount Zion, and unto the city of the living God, the heavenly Jerusalem" (Heb. 12:22).

"For here we have no continuing city, but we seek one to come" (Heb. 13:14).

"The holy city, new Jerusalem" (Rev. 21:2).
Think of the

Cities of the Bible

In the Bible we find the names of many cities. "Cain . . . builded a city, and called the name of the city, after the name of his son, Enoch" (Gen. 4:17). "Asshur . . . builded Nineveh and the city Rehoboth, and Calah" (10:11).

Dwellers in the land of Shinar (11:2) said: "Let us build us a city" (v. 4). "And the Lord came down to see the city and the tower, which the children of men builded" (v. 5).

Note the mention of some cities. "The name of the city was called Zoar" (19:22).

The Lord spoke of the cities of Sodom and Gomorrah as grievously sinful (18:20).

"He . . . went unto the city of Nahor" (24:10).

"The name of the city was Beer-sheba" (26:33).

"The name of that city was called Luz" (28:19).

"Jacob came to Shalem, a city of Shechem" (33:18).

"And the name of the city was Dinhabah" (36:32).

"And the name of the city was Avith" (36:35).

"And the name of the city was Pau" (36:39).

"Heshbon was the city of Sihon the king" (Num. 21:26).

"Jericho, the city of palm trees" (Deut. 34:3).

"And Nibshan, and the city of Salt, and En-gedi" (Josh. 15:62).

"Kirjath-jearim, a city" (18:14).

"The strong city of Tyre" (19:29).

"And the name of the city was called Hormah" (Judg. 1:17).

"They called the name of the city Dan" (18:29).

"The name of the city was Laish" (18:29).

"[They] buried him in Ramah, even in his own city" (1 Sam. 28:3).

"The king of the city of Sepharvaim" (2 Kings 19:13).

Bethezel—in the north of Judah.

Nineveh was an exceeding great city.

The city of David.

The city of Bethsaida.

The city of Lasea.

The city of Sychar.

"City of waters"—name given by Joab to part of Rabbah, the chief city of the Ammonites.

"City of confusion is broken down" is a symbolic name for Jerusalem.

"Great city of Babylon."

"A city called Nain."

Imperial city of Rome.

City of Athens—"drunk with the wine of skepticism."

Ephesus.

Tarsus.

Damascus.

"City of David." That part of Jerusalem built on Mount Zion. "Zion: the same is of the city of David" (2 Sam. 5:7). "City of David" mentioned thirty times.

Athens mentioned often.

"They brought him [Paul] unto Athens" (Acts 17:15).

"Now when Paul waited for them at Athens" (Acts 17:16).

"Then Paul . . . said, Ye men of Athens" (Acts 17:22).

"After these things Paul departed from Athens" (Acts 18:1).

"We thought it good to be left at Athens alone" (1 Thess. 3:1).

ROME:

"Strangers of Rome, Jews and proselytes" (Acts 2:10).

"I must also see Rome" (Acts 19:21).

"So must thou bear witness also at Rome" (Acts 23:11).

"To all that be in Rome, beloved of God" (Rom. 1:7).

"I am ready to preach the gospel to you that are at Rome" (Rom. 1:15).

"When he was in Rome, he sought me out" (2 Tim.

1:17).

CORINTH:

Paul lived here eighteen months.

We read: "Paul . . . came to Corinth" (Acts 18:1).

"The church of God which is at Corinth"

"Erastus abode at Corinth."

BETHLEHEM:

"Joseph . . . went . . . unto the city of David, which is called Bethlehem" (Luke 2:4).

Bethlehem called a town often. Only once is it called a city.

Here heaven put out its brightest star to mark Jesus' birthplace—when he came down from his glory, down from the heights of Deity to the depths of humanity.

JERUSALEM:

Means "possession of peace." It is fifteen miles from Jordan River and Dead Sea and thirty-one miles from Mediterranean Sea.

Built on four hills—Zion, Acra, Moriah, Bezetha, it is surrounded on east, west, south by a valley which was environed with hills.

It had three walls with towers and was about four and one-half miles in circumference.

During 1011-1004 B.C., its Temple was built.

In 970 it was plundered by Shishak.

In 884 it was plundered by the Philistines and Arabs.

In 710, beseiged by Sennacherib.

In 610, taken by Pharaoh Necho.

In 598, plundered by Nebuchadnezzar.

In 587, the Temple was burned.

In 538 Cyrus encouraged its rebuilding.

In 515 it was dedicated.

In 445 Nehemiah rebuilt the walls.

In 332 visited by Alexander the Great.
In 320 captured by Ptolemy Sater.
In 302 annexed to Egypt.
In 170 its walls were torn down by Antiochus Epiphanes.
In 65, taken by Pompey.
In 44 the wall was rebuilt by Antipas, father of Herod the Great.
In A.D. 70 it was destroyed by the Romans.
In 130 rebuilt by Hadrian.
In 335 Constantine founded the Church of the Holy Sepulchre.
In 614, taken by the Persians.
In 637, taken by the Saracens.
In 1076, taken by the Turks.
In 1087, taken by Saladin.
In 1098, assigned to Egypt.
In 1099, taken by the Crusaders.
In 1228, assigned to the Christians.
In 1243, taken by the Carizimians.
In 1517, taken by the Ottomans.
In 1832, assigned to Egypt.
In 1841, assigned to Turkey.
In 1917, taken peaceably by General Allenby.
Think now of

Some Cities of the World

London—with its fog and smoke and royal family.
Moscow—with its cold winters—once with its czars and now with its communism advocacy.
Paris—with its Seine River and Napoleon's tomb and Eiffel Tower and Victor Hugo's mausoleum.
Berlin—with its war scars and Kaiser and Hitler.
Rome—with its antiquities and Colosseum and cruelties

and Nero.

Madrid—chief city of a nation whose piratical ships once harrassed all seas and filled the nation's coffers with gold.

Edinburgh—with its universities and John Knox who said: "Give me Scotland or I die."

Boston—with its Bunker Hill and Tea Party.

Yorktown—with its surrender of Cornwallis.

Philadelphia—city of brotherly love and Independence Hall.

Washington, D. C.—with our nation's Capitol.

Charleston, S. C.—with its ancient lore and superb culture and naval base.

Saint Petersburg, Florida—with its old streets.

New Orleans—most interesting city in the world.

Chicago—noted for schools and underworld characters.

San Francisco—remembered for its earthquake and fire.

Los Angeles—with more "isms" that ought to become "wasms" than any city in America.

Galveston—with its flood of 1900.

Miami—lovely with beauty often ravished by harrowing hurricanes.

Calcutta and Bombay—filled with hunger and beggars— in India with its Hinduism and cow worship.

Istanbul—noted for dirt and devotion to Islamism.

New York—with a variety of many things good and many things bad—where, out of eight million population, six and one-half million have no religious affiliation of any kind. Great hurrying, scurrying, worrying New York—with many thousands on welfare rolls.

But, in all these cities I have mentioned and in many other cities of other nations I do not mention—

Not one is free of dirt and disease.

Not one is free of sorrow and broken hearts.

Not one is free of sin and shame.

Not one is free of despair and death.

Not one is free of fear of war and destruction.

Not one can be assured no storm will ever assault.

Not one can be assured that no earthquake will ever make it tremble and know destruction.

Not one can be assured it will never have an epidemic of some dread disease.

Not one can be assured that no fire of conflagration proportions will ever burn and wreak havoc.

In all these cities beggars—hungry and haggard; and ambulances for the sick and those maimed in accidents; and hospitals for the sick and suffering; and funeral processions and cemeteries; and jails and police courts; and crime and law-breaking and defiance of civil authority; and many women belonging to the scarlet sisterhood of the streets—dirty toys of evil-minded and lustful men; and saloons—dispensing liquid damnation that blights individuals, planting the seeds of dissolution and misery in many homes, and lowering the moral tones of communities.

In all these cities are unwed mothers and illegitimate children, are the blind who never see a sunset or a starry sky, are the deaf who never hear the boom of thunder in a storm cloud or the dash of rain on window panes or the song of birds or the laughter of children.

In all these cities are the crippled—helpless to walk without crutches or to go without wheelchairs; and are funeral processions—with hearses slowly nodding dark plumes to some cemetery.

In all these cities broken families and disregard of the decencies of life—evil men and women who do evil intensely with both hands.

In all these cities, there is the stink of unrighteousness

instead of the sweet smell of righteousness; human fears and furies, vice and hatred and devilishness and harlotry and hypocrisy and the works of the flesh.

Of all these cities not one is PERMANENT.

The Bible says: "For here we have no continuing city" (Heb. 13:14).

And the apostle John, writing in the wisdom and power of the Holy Spirit, describes the foundations of this holy city.

"And the building of the wall of it was of jasper: and the city was pure gold, like unto clear glass. And the foundations of the wall of the city were garnished with all manner of precious stones. The first foundation was jasper; the second, sapphire; the third, a chalcedony; the fourth, an emerald;

"The fifth, sardonyx; the sixth, sardius; the seventh, chrysolyte; the eighth, beryl; the ninth, a topaz; the tenth, a chrysoprasus; the eleventh, a jacinth; the twelfth, an amethyst.

"And the twelve gates were twelve pearls: every several gate was of one pearl: and the street of the city was pure gold, as it were transparent glass" (Rev. 21:18-21).

Yes—a city concerning which Paul wrote: "But ye are come unto mount Zion, and unto the city of the living God, the heavenly Jerusalem, and to an innumerable company of angels" (Heb. 12:22).

Yes—the great and holy city about which the apostle John by the Holy Spirit wrote: "And I John saw the holy city, new Jerusalem, coming down from God out of heaven, prepared as a bride adorned for her husband" (Rev. 21:2).

We learn that now there are large associations such as the International City Planning Firm, a System Development Center of Washington, D. C., and a System Development Corporation of California which are definitely concerned about improving the conditions of our cities.

They claim that by mobilizing science, they are dealing with dynamically growing systems—the cities—and in this concept they are heading toward the universal city—in every country in the world.

No doubt much can be done to improve the conditions in our cities—and the efforts of these benevolently minded and intelligent people will be greatly rewarded, and their results enjoyed by many.

But one of these associations' administrators realized and acknowledged that "a complete city—a perfect city—will never be built." What man is unable to do—with all his legislature and educational institutions and scientific power—God *can* do and *has* done. "[God] hath prepared for them a city" (Heb. 11:16). "[Abraham] looked for a city whose builder and maker is God" (Heb. 11:10).

And in due time, this heavenly city will be revealed.

The apostle John wrote about "one of the seven angels" who showed him "that great city, the holy Jerusalem" (Rev. 21:9-10).

Let us notice carefully

The Perfection of This City

1. *It is perfectly perfect in its establishment.*

For it has twelve foundations. "And the wall of the city had twelve foundations, and in them the names of the twelve apostles of the Lamb" (Rev. 21:14).

2. *It is perfectly perfect in its accessibility.*

For it has twelve gates—three for each side. "And had a wall great and high, and had twelve gates, and at the gates twelve angels, and names written thereon, which are the names of the twelve tribes of the children of Israel: On the east three gates; on the north three gates; on the south three gates; and on the west three gates" (Rev. 21:12-13).

These gates shall never be closed.

3. *It is perfectly perfect in its purity.*

"And there shall in no wise enter into it any thing that defileth, neither whatsoever worketh abomination; or maketh a lie: but they which are written in the Lamb's book of life" (Rev. 21:27).

4. *It is perfection as to its illumination.*

"And the city had no need of the sun, neither of the moon, to shine in it; for the glory of God did lighten it, and the Lamb is the light thereof" (Rev. 21:23).

5. *It is perfection as to its beauty.*

"Having the glory of God: and her light was like unto a stone most precious, even like a jasper stone, clear as crystal" (Rev. 21:11).

Each gate is a pearl—and the light is like unto a stone most precious, even a jasper stone, clear as crystal.

6. *It is perfection as to its spaciousness.*

As many have told us through the years, the great city wherein is our Father's house, our future home, that city with equal length and width and height, is fifteen hundred miles long, fifteen hundred miles high, fifteen hundred miles wide. That means, as many preachers have told us, that in that great and glorious city there are streets over streets and stories over stories up, up, up to the height of fifteen hundred miles—and each street fifteen hundred miles long.

This city of God is a solid cube of golden construction fifteen hundred miles every way. One scholarly writer wrote: "The base of this city would stretch from fartherest

Maine to fartherest Florida and from the Atlantic to Colorado. It would cover all of Ireland, Britain, France, Spain, Italy, Germany, Austria, most of Turkey, and half of European Russia taken together. Marvelous this city of gold whose every street is one third of the diameter of the earth. The number of main avenues, one mile above each other and a mile apart, would total eight million miles.

"And we are assured that this city has a capacity for more people than could be born on this earth in 10,000 years, for it is estimated that every human being from Adam until now, if they were all saved, would hardly fill one corner of this enormous structure."

7. *This city is perfection as to its administration.* "And there shall be no more curse: but the throne of God and of the Lamb shall be in it; and his servants shall serve him" (Rev. 22:3).

In heaven there is perfect *security.* "There shall be no more curse" (Rev. 22:3). The curse came because of sin. Sin will no more invade the province of God.

In heaven there is perfect *government.* "The throne of God and the Lamb shall be in it" (Rev. 22:3). Since the fall of man, the human race has been cursed by misgovernment. That will be ended forever.

In heaven there is perfect *service.* "His servants shall serve him" (Rev. 22:3). What the nature of that service is we do not know. But we do know that it will please God and all who serve.

In heaven there is perfect *fellowship.* "They shall see his face" (Rev. 22:4). Sweeter than the joys of lovers at the trysting place will be your fellowship with the faithful God "by whom ye were called into the fellowship of his Son Jesus Christ our Lord" (1 Cor. 1:9).

In heaven there is perfect *recognition.* "His name shall

be in their foreheads" (Rev. 22:4). We shall not know less in heaven than we know here. "Now we see through a glass, darkly, but then face to face: . . . then shall I know even as also I am known" (1 Cor. 13:12). We may confidently expect to know every person in heaven.

In heaven there is perfect *knowledge.* "The Lord God giveth them light" (Rev. 22:5). "We know in part. . . . But when that which is perfect is come, then that which is in part shall be done away" (1 Cor. 13:10).

In heaven there is perfect *victory.* "They shall reign for ever and ever" (Rev. 22:5). There is no defeat by the world; there is no defeat by the devil; there is no defeat by the flesh. May God make "us meet to be partakers of the inheritance of the saints in light" (Col. 1:12).

I say again that madness it is, utter insanity, for a man to miss heaven. I think Talmadge must have meant that when he said that the only proper epitaph for a lost man, for a man who misses heaven, is: "Thou fool."

How glorious to know that, as Paul wrote: "But as it is written, Eye hath not seen, nor ear heard, neither have entered into the heart of man, the things which God hath prepared for them that love him" (1 Cor. 2:9).

This city of such indescribable perfection will be the residence of the bride of the Lamb.

The Lamb is the Lord Jesus Christ. "But with the precious blood of Christ, as of a lamb without blemish and without spot" (1 Pet. 1:19).

And the bride is composed of all born-again believers—called "the church of the firstborn which are written in heaven"—the Lamb's book of life.

> "But ye are come unto mount Zion, and unto the city of the living God, the heavenly Jerusalem, and to an innumerable company of angels, "To the general

assembly and church of the firstborn, which are written in heaven, and to God the Judge of all, and to the spirits of just men made perfect" (Heb. 12:22-23).

There is the Lamb's book of life.

"And there shall in no wise enter into it any thing that defileth, neither whatsoever worketh abomination, or maketh a lie: but they which are written in the Lamb's book of life" (Rev. 21:27).

This book contains a perfect record of all persons who are trusting in the perfect sacrifice of the Lamb of God.

The Lord told his disciples to rejoice because their names were written in heaven. "Notwithstanding in this rejoice not, that the spirits are subject unto you; but rather rejoice, because your names are written in heaven" (Luke 10:20).

Is your name written there—on the page white and fair?

The only way to be sure of this is through Christ Jesus, who is *Perfection to the uttermost.*

Think of the Master in heaven—the one Star in brightness and beauty above all other stars. Giving loving thought to the Master—the one to whom God has given a name above every name, not only in this world but in the world to come. Give grateful consideration to the Master—who is wisdom, in action, in affection is "the fairest among ten thousand, the one altogether lovely."

Let us remember and rejoice to remember that the light of heaven is the face of Jesus, that the joy of heaven is the service of Jesus, that the fullness of heaven is the name of Jesus, that the harmony of heaven is the praise of Jesus, that the theme of heaven is the work of Jesus, that the employment of heaven is the service of Jesus, that the fullness of heaven is Jesus himself, that the duration of heaven is the eternity of Jesus.

The Master—once cursed on earth, now crowned in heaven.

The Master—once in humiliation on earth, now in exaltation in heaven.

The Master—once in agony on earth, now adored in heaven.

The Master—once despised of men on earth, now worshipped by angels in heaven.

The Master—once the victim in the gory place on earth, now the victor in the glory place of heaven.

The Master—once in the land of graves on earth, now in the graveless land—heaven.

And this heaven and the joys of it and the blessedness of it are eternal.

Acknowledge your sins!

Acknowledge Jesus as Savior and Lord—and go rejoicing on your way to this four-square eternal city, which all the words of the wisest of men, most skillfully combined and most eloquently spoken or written cannot fully describe.

8.
From Death unto Life

"From death unto life" (John 5:24; 1 John 3:14).

In 1888, sixty-five hundred persons died of diphtheria in New York State. But the dreaded wings of diphtheria that fluttered above many cradles and darkened many homes have been clipped and death thwarted. The medical helplessness of that awful time is no more—mainly because of Robert Koch who died in 1910, sixty-seven years old. He is famous for his postulates that revolutionized the concepts of disease and its treatment. His bacteria studies, far more thorough and definitive than those of Pasteur, made him famous. Many today who know of his researches give thanks to Koch for his work of incalculable benefit to mankind—against diseases that ravaged the world.

In a world where sin is rampant and ruinous how much more abundant should be the thanks of millions for the chance to have salvation—to pass from death to life through the Lord Jesus Christ.

Jesus, who spoke as never man spoke, said:

He that honoureth not the Son honoureth not the Father which hath sent him. . . . He that heareth my

word and believeth on him that sent me, hath everlasting life, and shall not come into condemnation;
but is passed from death unto life (John 5:23-24).

Paul, who compassed the known earth with the truths
of redemption, said: "You hath he made alive, when you
were dead . . . in sins" (Eph. 2:1).

John, the beloved apostle, wrote: "We know we have
passed from death unto life" (1 John 3:14).

Death

But Jesus and John and Paul speak not in these words
of bodily and temporal death—of that death whose only
pleasure fountains are falling tears, whose only light is
darkness, whose only gold is bones scattered at the grave's
mouth, whose only palace is a huge skull. For saved and
unsaved die that physical death—finding no exemption
from this debt of nature. Jesus, John, and Paul mean *spiritual* death—ending in *eternal* death, the death of soul and
body, the dreadful destruction Christ taught men to fear,
saying: "Fear not them which kill the body, but are not
able to kill the soul: but rather fear him which is able
to destroy both soul and body in hell" (Matt. 10:28), the
death which ultimately is going away into the "everlasting
fire, prepared for the devil and his angels"—"punished
with everlasting destruction from the presence of the
Lord," the endurance of "the wrath of the Lamb"—death
with its sting unremoved!

> "There is a death whose pang
> Outlasts the fleeting breath,
> Oh, what eternal terrors hang
> Around the second death.
> Lord God of Truth and Grace,

Teach us that death to shun,
Lest we be banished from Thy face.
And evermore undone."

Paul said: "You, being *dead* in your sins" (Col. 2:13).

This means that men, their souls brought "into captivity to the law of sin"—evil hearts, unholy passions, depraved affections predominating—are outside of Christ's saving mercy—dead by means of sin and their sins. This fearful statement—universal in rule since Adam fell—means that sinners impenitent, hating not sin, loving not God, not acquitted in Christ, not made perfectly righteous through faith in Christ, not washed in Christ's blood, the eyes of their souls not directed toward the cross, having never come to Christ, refusing to come to Christ that they might have life (John 10:10), never having experienced a sense of reconciliation, their natural enmity toward God stubbornly maintained, are as dead as entombed Lazarus before the voice of Jesus summoned him. Spiritually dead, though naturally alive.

The unregenerate man is spiritually dead without Christ. His soul in its unredeemed state is under the power of sin, the curse of the law, the influence of the present world, the frivolous habits of life, and other spiritual enemies. Dead is he to well-founded hope and to the covenant of grace. Without Christ as Savior by faith—dead. Dead, though respectable. Dead, though honored of men. Dead, though positioned in places of political power. Dead, though educated and cultured. Dead, though decent, exemplary, and satisfied with outer forms of outward godliness. Dead because he has rejected God's Son as Savior—excusing himself from accepting gospel invitations, alibiing himself into hell. Dead—the moral sense so perverted that all wonders of grace, all excellencies of Christ

which the cross reveals, all warnings and promises of the
Bible fall upon him "like sunbeams upon the eyes of the
dead." Though alive physically, as dead under the damning
sentence of the law, as dead in respect to the privileges
and promotions of spiritual life, as dead in opposition to
regeneration and sanctification, as dead in insensibility to
spiritual and heavenly things as the dead in their graves
to earthly noise. Dead from two causes—the ignorance
which men inherit from the fall, and the law of sin in
the members which leads to actual rebellion against God.

Dead are unsaved men to Christ and to "God . . . in
Christ, reconciling the world unto himself"—no faith in
him; no response to his love; no felt need of his mercy;
no recognition in their hearts of the criminality of their
sins; no acknowledgment of the terrible liabilities and
dangerous consequences of sin; no repentance unto eternal
life; no awareness that all unforgiven sin will be accom-
panied with an absolutely righteous retribution; no belief
that Jesus, the wisest and tenderest who ever appeared
on earth, who loved and lived and died as none other,
was neither afraid nor ashamed to speak the truth about
hell.

Their aliveness in the body is described by Job: "They
take the timbrel and harp. . . . They spend their days
in wealth, and in a moment go down to the grave. Therefore they say unto God, Depart from us; for we desire
not the knowledge of thy ways. What is the Almighty,
that we should serve him? and what profit should we have,
if we pray unto him?" (Job 21:12-15).

A man may be blind and alive, deaf and alive, dumb
and alive. But if he is insensible to material things, he
is dead. So it is with the unrenewed soul; it meets all
objects and agencies of the spiritual world with cold indif-

ference, with utter unconcern. Though he is charged with numerous transgressions and the wrath of God abides on him, he is sensible of no burden. Though destruction and misery are in his ways, he is unalarmed. Though God reproves, encourages, asserts His authority, displays the reasonableness of His command, addresses man's hope and man's fear, draws back the veil that hides the eternal world and sets life and death, blessing and cursing before them, men turn away from Him that speaketh, reject the counsel of God against themselves, remaining stubbornly inflexible against all God's overtures of love and mercy.

Spiritually dead "the wide world through" is the natural man—completely devoid of natural life. Alive worldward, alive selfward, alive sinward, but dead Godward. Men who are alive physically, whose souls have union with their bodies, understand natural things. They reason, talk, contrive, play, work, eat, drink, marry, build, plant, trade—and receive the natural benefits of such. But their souls, having no union with Christ, are in the state and power of spiritual death. There is no motion toward God and heavenly things. Though many excellencies adorn their associations with men, those excellencies are so many flowers on a corpse. Their affections toward God are frozen—as lifeless toward Christ as fleshly skeletons. Such is the sad, deplorable deadness of the unsaved individual, the unsaved hosts, the unregenerate world.

Note the

Cause of This Death

Sin, enmity against God, his attributes, and God's government which would depose God from his sovereignty, is the cause of this dreadful death. "Sin . . . slew me" (Rom. 7:11). "The wages of sin is death" (Rom. 6:23).

"Dead in your sins" (Col. 2:13). "Sin hath reigned unto death" (Rom. 5:21). "Sin, when it is finished, bringeth forth death" (Jas. 1:15).

Sin, in destruction extensive, makes universal abuse of Christ's person, nature, offices, his righteousness, his blood, his death. Sin—awful, universal, inescapable—the quintessence of all horrors, the causative element of all world suffering, ghastly great among life's factors, throws man, woefully deranged, miserable, ungoverned, erratic, lost, into blackness.

Sin, the most terrible fact of God's universe, life's most dreadful and inexorable curse, manifest inwardly in discrowned faculties and degradation of human love and brutalized spirits, is the skull set amidst life's banquet, the desert breath that drinks every dew—a madness in the brain, a poison in the heart, an opiate in the will, a frenzy in the imagination.

Sin, the disease of the soul, the instrument of everlasting ruin, the midnight blackness that invests man's whole moral being, subverted the constitutional order of man's nature, dismantled him of his nobility, caused him to give unconditional surrender to diabolical power, destroyed the harmony of his powers.

Sin, destructive of all happiness, ruining men, ruining angels, has withered everything fair.

Sin, darkening the understanding, searing the conscience, making the will rebellious, occasioning all tears of sorrow and all pangs of agony, has blasted everything good, made bitter everything sweet, rolled tides of tragedy far and wide—sweeping all lands with death.

Sin, promising velvet and giving a shroud, promising liberty and giving slavery, promising nectar and giving gall, promising good fruit and giving the cast-out rinds of carousal; promising perfumed handkerchiefs and giving foul rags, promising silk and giving sackcloth, provides only mimic crowns and ghostly garlands.

Sin's gold has no purchasing power. Sin's revelry is burlesque, sin's splendors faded spangles, sin's pleasures ghastly fictions.

But, let us ask through whom and by whom do we pass from death unto life? To that question there is only one answer—now and forever. The answer is

Jesus Christ

From a condition so utterly corrupt, from the death so to be dreaded, how is the lost sinner to be rescued? the diseased soul cured? the captive made free? the dead made alive? By puny articulations of human eloquence? by arts of speech? by improvement of environment? by culture? Can the influence of moral suasion affect this work? No. These things are as impotent to bring this rescue from death to life, from bondage to liberty, from rottenness to health, from the pit to the throne, from the depths of ruin untold, as is an infant's arm to chain the lightning, as is a teaspoon to stay the mad plunge of an avalanche. But in Christ is this rescue, this life, this health, this liberty.

There is no way but in the sacrificial death of Jesus who "appeared to put away sin by the sacrifice of himself" (Heb. 9:26), and to whom is given the only name "under heaven . . . among men, whereby we must be saved" (Acts 4:12). And this remedy, this rescue, this being made alive from the dead in the sacrificial death of Christ is available by faith—because through Christ "is preached unto you the forgiveness of sins: and by him all that believe are justified from all things from which ye could not be justified by the law of Moses" (Acts 13:38-39).

"The law of the Spirit of life in Christ Jesus hath made
me free from the law of sin and death" (Rom. 8:2). Only
Christ Jesus is the everlasting source of human salvation.
He only, by a work consistent with the character of God,
can break the power which holds us in chains, avert punishment which threatens us, fortify with fresh sanctions
the law which we have broken, and reconciling justice
with mercy, open to mankind the fountains of grace.
Through him the law is vindicated, the holiness of God
doubly honored, and mercy in richest munificence proclaimed to the sinner.

The God of all grace poured out wrath upon the sinless
Christ. Forsaken was he that our sins might be forgiven
and forgotten. He received the wages of sin which he never
earned that we might have eternal life which we never
deserved. To the bottom of the pit went he that we might
be in the bosom of the Father. Christ, the mercy seat for
the whole world, found no mercy for himself. He went
into awful gloom that we might enter into glory. Sold was
he that we might ransomed be. Denied was he that he
might confess us to the Father. Bound was he that he might
bestow on us true freedom—the freedom of sons. Unjustly
judged was he that we might escape the severity of God's
judgments. Scourged was he that by his stripes we might
be healed. "For he hath made him to be sin for us, who
knew no sin; that we might be made the righteousness
of God in him" (2 Cor. 5:21).

Meaning what? Meaning that on the cross Jesus became
for you, for me, for every man, all that the holy and just
God must judge that we, through faith in him, might
become all that God cannot judge. Meaning that on the
cross, Jesus the perfectly righteous one was judged as
unrighteous that we, the unrighteous sinners, through faith

in him, might be judged as righteous. Meaning that on the cross he stood before God with all of our sins upon himself that we might stand before God with none of our sins upon ourselves. Meaning that on the cross God, in our behalf, dealt with Jesus as he must deal with sin—in severe and unrelenting judgment.

What will you do with this Christ in whom are all the riches of grace?—whose arms are never closed against penitence?—who went through the gates of death that the gates of death might never hold you in. He lay in your grave that you might sit on his throne. He "brought immortality to light through the gospel." He bore your sins in his own body on the tree. What will you do with him?

Even though the portals of hell are open and you have lifted your foot to step inside, if you will turn around and cry unto him for divine forgiveness, the salvation that found Jonah in the depths of the sea, the soiled woman at Jacob's well, the rich Zacchaeus in his home, the dying thief on the cross, will find you at the mouth of hell. The Savior—able, willing, mighty to save—stands ready to bring you from death to life. No reluctance, but only highest willingness is on his side. You can pass from death to life through him. What will you do with him who was assaulted that you might be acquitted?—smitten that you might be healed?—lacerated that you might be liberated?—slain that you might be saved?—who met all tortures of condemnation for your justification?—and who some day will change the whole world by the brightness of his coming?

Therefore, as a lost and guilty sinner, claim the sinner's Savior. Rest your all on Christ's work for you, not on your works for him. Say:

"In my hand no price I bring,
Simply to Thy cross I cling."

—Augustus M. Toplady

Then you will pass from death to life.

9.
The Grace
of God

"For the grace of God that bringeth salvation hath appeared to all men" (Titus 2:11).

"Grace . . . came by Jesus Christ" (John 1:17).

The word *grace* blossoms often in the Bible's garden of truths.

The word *grace* shines like a radiant star in the sky of the Scriptures.

The word *grace* flows like a deep, pure river in the continent of Bible assertions.

The word *grace* sounds forth like the music of many choirs in one anthem in the orchestra of Bible revelation.

The many times the word *grace* appears in the Bible is for sinners' souls like rain upon drought-smitten fields.

The word *grace*, as we read it in the Bible, is like balm for sin-bruised hearts.

The word *grace*, as it is found in the Bible, is like a key that opens jail doors and lets sinners under death sentence go free.

As to the grace of God, let us consider some statements.

Some have made statements in their attempt to give

definitions of the grace of God.

Difficult it is to take a word used as many times and
with such a diversity of application. Difficult it is to com-
press into one sentence the meaning of the doctrine of
grace—one of the divine perfections of God which is exercised in the salvation of sinners. Great, dedicated, scholarly
men have acknowledged a woeful sense of inadequacy
as they have tried to give descriptions and definitions of
it.

My own definition of the grace of God is this: the
unlimited and unmerited favor given to the utterly undeserving. Dr. Dole says: "Grace is love which passes
beyond all claims to love." Alexander Whyte wrote: "Grace
and love are essentially the same, only grace is love mani-
festing itself and operating under certain conditions, and
addressing itself to certain circumstances. As, for example,
love has no limit or law such as grace has. Love may exist
between equals, or it may rise to those above us, or flow
down to those in any way beneath us. But grace has only
one direction it can take. Grace always flows down, and
thus it is that God's love to sinners is always called grace."

Alexander Maclaren declared: "The word *grace* is a kind
of shorthand for the whole sum of unmerited blessings
which come to men through Jesus Christ. GRACE means
the unconditioned, undeserved, spontaneous, eternal,
stooping, pardoning love of God."

The author, Phillips: "Grace is something in God which
is at the heart of all His redeeming activities, the downward
stoop and reach of God, bending from the height of His
majesty to touch and grasp our insignificance and poverty."

C. D. Cole says: "God's disposition of love and favor
toward a sinner is grace."

Grace is "A comprehensive word of boundless reach and

an infinite depth of significance, signifying unlimited favor to the undeserving, all who by reason of transgression forfeited every claim to Divine favor, and have lost all capacity for meritorious action" (Butler).

Think now of the severals of grace.

By that I mean that the word *grace* sometimes refers to a gift and sometimes to power, but even then it contains the element of unmerited favor.

Grace is unmerited favor. It means that we get just the opposite of what we deserve.

There is *saving* grace. The grace of God has brought salvation. "The grace of God that bringeth salvation" (Titus 2:11).

And salvation is Jesus. "Thou shalt call his name JESUS: for he shall save his people from their sins" (Matt. 1:21).

It is Jesus who saves. It is Jesus who keeps. "The grace of God . . . hath appeared to all men" (Titus 2:11).

But only those who receive it are saved.

> "For if by one man's offence death reigned by one, much more they which receive abundance of grace and of the gift of righteousness shall reign in life by one, Jesus Christ" (Rom. 5:17).

> "And he said unto Jesus, Lord, remember me when thou comest into thy kingdom. And Jesus said unto him, Verily I say unto thee, To day shalt thou be with me in paradise" (Luke 23:42-43).

By God's grace sinners are called. "But when it pleased God, who . . . called me by his grace" (Gal. 1:15).

By God's grace, sinners are saved. "But we believe that through the grace of the Lord Jesus Christ we shall be saved" (Acts 15:11).

By the grace of God, sinners are redeemed and forgiven.

"In whom we have redemption through his blood, the forgiveness of sins, according to the riches of his grace" (Eph. 1:7).

By God's grace, sinners are justified freely. "Being justified freely by his grace, through the redemption that is in Christ Jesus" (Rom. 3:24).

By the grace of God, sinners are accepted in the Beloved. "To the praise of the glory of his grace, wherein he hath made us accepted in the beloved" (Eph. 1:6).

By the grace of God, sinners are raised and seated in the heavenlies.

"God . . . even when we were dead in sins, hath quickened us together with Christ (by grace ye are saved;) and hath raised us up together, and made us sit together in heavenly places in Christ Jesus: that in the ages to come he might show the exceeding riches of his grace in his kindness toward us through Christ Jesus" (Eph. 2:4-7).

By the grace of God, sinners are given everlasting consolation and good hope.

"Now our Lord Jesus Christ himself, and God, even our Father, which hath loved us, and hath given us everlasting consolation and good hope through grace, comfort your hearts" (2 Thess. 2:16-17).

By the grace of God, we are given boldness in prayer. "Let us therefore come boldly unto the throne of grace, that we may obtain mercy, and find grace to help in time of need" (Heb. 4:16).

By the grace of God, we are kept in victory and enabled to glorify the name of our Lord Jesus Christ. "That the name of our Lord Jesus Christ may be glorified in you, and ye in him, according to the grace of our God and the Lord Jesus Christ" (2 Thess. 1:12).

By the grace of God, we are shown kindness. "Shew the exceeding riches of his grace in his kindness toward us through Jesus Christ" (Eph. 2:7).

By the grace of God, we are made to inherit promises. "It is of faith, that it might be by grace; to the end that the promise might be sure to all" (Rom. 4:16).

By the grace of God, we are helped to serve God. "Let us have grace, whereby we may serve God acceptably with reverence and godly fear" (Heb. 12:28).

By the grace of God, we are given power to behave in the world as children of God. "Not with fleshly wisdom, but by the grace of God, we have had our conversation in the world, and more abundantly to you-ward" (2 Cor. 1:12).

By the grace of God, we are given joy in liberality.

"The grace of God bestowed on the churches of Macedonia; How that in a great trial of affliction the abundance of their joy and their deep poverty abounded with the riches of their liberality" (2 Cor. 8:1-2).

Let us think of the strength of grace.

Sin is very powerful in this world. Sin is powerful as an opiate in the will. Sin is powerful as a frenzy in the imagination. Sin is powerful as a poison in the heart. Sin is powerful as a madness in the brain. Sin is powerful as a desert breath that drinks up all spiritual dews. Sin is powerful as the sum of all terrors. Sin is powerful as the quintessence of all horrors. Sin is powerful to devastate, to doom, to damn.

"The wages of sin is death" (Rom. 6:23).

Sin, the aggregation of all evils, the quintessence of all horrors, entered the world. And death, the sum of all penalties, by sin (Rom. 5:12). Soon graves were digged in the earth. Soon there were empty places in households. Eve washing Abel's dead face with tears. Sarah buried in Ephron; Rachel buried in Ephrath. Abraham laid to rest beside Sarah. Jacob on his last journey. Joseph in a coffin in Egypt. David in a tomb. Solomon in a shroud. Ever since the funeral journey has never ceased. Well-trodden the road that leads to the grave—a hard path, solid as lead, without a flower in all its weary miles. Yes! Death passed upon all men—because all men have sinned.

But the grace of God is more powerful than sin. "Where sin abounded, grace did much more abound" (Rom. 5:20).

Here is the sinner's only hope, although, until quickened by the Spirit of grace, he does not know it. No man can rescue himself from the tyranny of sin. Men may reform, but they cannot regenerate themselves. Men may give up their crimes and their vices, but they cannot, by their own strength, give up their sins. Can the Ethiopian change his skin? No. Can the leopard eliminate his spots? No.

Sin abounded unto Paradise but grace abounds unto Paradise regained.

Sin abounded unto man's "shameful failure and loss." Grace abounds unto man's eternal riches in Christ.

> "All that He has
> He shares with them
> Who, trusting Him, they make confessions.
> Redeemed from sin
> They enter in
> To all He wrought for their possession."

Without the intervention of saving grace the gates of

mercy would have been forever closed. "That as sin hath reigned unto death, even so might GRACE reign through righteousness unto eternal life by Jesus Christ our Lord" (Rom. 5:21).

In all the sixty-five hundred hymns Charles Wesley wrote, I doubt if there are any sweeter words than these:

> "Plenteous grace with Thee is found,
> Grace to cover all my sin."

Judas Iscariot was "one of the twelve." There is God's orchestra. "He . . . hanged himself." There is hell's laughter.

"Now this man purchased a field with the reward of iniquity; and falling headlong, he burst asunder in the midst, and all his bowels gushed out" (Acts 1:18).

Instead of hanging himself, Judas Iscariot might have done one of three things. He might have, as one has written, attempted a rescue on the way to Calvary—and died on the point of a Roman spear or with a Roman sword in his bowels. He might have invested his money and gained some more money from his iniquitous betrayal. He might have gone to Calvary and asked Jesus to forgive him. There at the cross mercy was waiting.

Oh, I wish he had gone to Jesus and begged mercy and forgiveness. I do. With all my heart, I do. With all my soul, I do. Then we would have had an eternally glorious exhibition of what Paul meant, who said: "Where sin abounded, grace did much more abound."

Judas showed, as my dear friend, William Russell Owen, put it, that sin is pitiless as poison, insidious as disease, and ruins like rot; that sin hates and hardens and hisses and hurts and hampers and hurls down to a heartless hell, that sin scoffs and scorns and satires and laughs and leers and lures and knifes and kills and damns and dooms and leaves man despairing and desolate, destitute and dead.

But had Judas sought mercy of Jesus at the cross, the world would have learned, as Russell Owen put it again, that the grace of God saves and seals and sanctifies and separates and makes superior, that grace consecrates and cleanses and changes and cures and crowns with the coronet of a king, that grace makes a pauper a prince, a prodigal a priest, and a castaway a queen; that grace sings a song when we sorrow, shouts a hallelujah when we die, sweeps us in a golden chariot beyond the farthest stars through the gates of pearl; that the grace of God clothes us in robes of righteousness, puts a crown on our head and sets man to stand before the throne of God a sinner saved and redeemed by the precious blood of Jesus.

We should think now of the source of grace.

The source of grace is the cross of Christ. "By grace are ye saved through faith; and not of yourselves: it is the gift of God" (Eph. 2:8).

The cross of Christ is the source of the grace of God.

"GRACE as fathomless as the sea,
GRACE flowing from Calvary."

—E. O. Excell

Grace did not have source in the irreproachable life of Christ. Nor in the marvelous teachings of Christ. Nor in the astonishing miracles of Christ.

The cross made grace possible.

Christ's cross at Calvary!

At Calvary all human sorrows hide in his wounds!

At Calvary the hieroglyphics of the types find their key.

At Calvary Satan's armor is removed.

At Calvary the fires of the law are extinguished.

At Calvary the penal claims of God against us are exhausted.

At Calvary every righteous judgment of God is perfectly met.

At Calvary our condemnation is lifted.

At Calvary the death of sin is made certain.

At Calvary our death sentence is revoked.

At Calvary the serpent's head is bruised.

At Calvary the door of heaven is opened.

At Calvary the fountain of salvation is unsealed.

At Calvary the world is stripped of its charms.

At Calvary the bitters of life are sweetened.

At Calvary the shadows of death are dispelled.

At Calvary the darkness of eternity is irradiated!

Now let us think as to *law* and *grace* of the *separation*.

Law is separate from grace—and grace from law.

Between them there is a vast chasm. How great the contrast between law and grace.

1. Origin: The law came by Moses—Grace and truth came by Jesus Christ (John 1:17).

2. Orders: The law says, "This do and live"—Grace says, "Live and then thou shalt do" (Phil. 2:13).

3. Demands: The law says: "Pay me that thou owest"—Grace says, "I frankly forgive thee all" (Compare Matt. 18:23-28; Luke 7:42).

4. Wages: The law says, "The soul that sinneth, it shall die" (Ezek. 18:4). Grace says: "He that believeth in me [Jesus], though he were dead, yet shall he live: and whosoever liveth and believeth in me shall never die" (John 11:25-26).

5. Death: The law says, "The soul that sinneth, it shall die" (Ezek. 18:4). Grace says: "He that believeth in me [Jesus], though he were dead, yet shall he live; and whosoever liveth and believeth in me shall never die"

(John 11:25-26).

6. Offers: The law pronounces condemnation and death (Gal. 3:10)—Grace proclaims justification and life (Rom. 5:1).

7. Heart: The law says, "Make you a new heart and a new spirit"—Grace says, "A new heart will I give you, and a new spirit will I put within you" (Ezek. 36:26).

8. Cursed and Blessed: The law says, "Cursed is every one that continueth not in all things" (Gal. 3:10)—Grace says, "Blessed is the man" (Rom. 4:8).

9. Love: The law says, "Thou shalt love the Lord thy God with all thy heart, all thy mind, all thy strength" (Deut. 6:5)—Grace says, "Herein is love" (1 John 4:10).

10. Doing: The law speaks of what men must do for God—Grace tells of what Christ has done for man (Eph. 2:10).

11. Creation: The law addresses man as a part of the old creation—Grace makes man a member of the new creation (2 Cor. 5:17).

12. Our Nature: The law bears on a nature prone to disobedience (Eph. 2:12)—Grace creates a nature inclined to obedience (Eph. 2:13).

13. Appeal: The law demands obedience by the terrors of the law—Grace beseeches men by the mercies of God (Rom. 12:1).

14. Holiness: The law demands holiness—Grace gives holiness.

15. God's Attitude: The law says, "Condemn him"—Grace says, "Embrace him." (Compare the prodigal son's return, the elder brother's attitude; the father's reception.)

16. Sacrifice: The law speaks of priestly sacrifices offered year by year, which could never make the comers thereunto perfect (Heb. 10:1)—Grace says, "But this man

. . ." (Heb. 10:2-12).

17. Judgment: The law declares that as many as have sinned in the law, shall be judged by the law—Grace brings eternal peace in defiance of the accusation (John 5:24).

Perhaps some repetition as I write from an old scrapbook some words I took down from a speaker in a Bible Conference—years ago.

In *The Evangel,* February 1961, I read this about law and grace:

The law says: The soul that sinneth, it shall die—Grace says: Whosoever believeth in Jesus, though he were dead, yet shall he live! and whosoever liveth and believeth in him shall never die.

The law pronounces condemnation and death—Grace proclaims justification and life.

The law says: Make you a new heart and a new spirit—Grace says: A new heart will I give you, and a new spirit will I put within you.

The law says: Cursed is every one that continueth not in all things which are written in the book of the law to do them—Grace says: Blessed is the man whose iniquities are forgiven, whose sin is covered; blessed is the man to whom God will not impute sin.

The law says: Thou shalt love the Lord thy God with all thy heart, and with all thy mind, and with all thy strength—Grace says: Herein is love, not that we loved God, but that he first loved us, and gave his Son to be the propitiation for our sins.

The law speaks of what man must do for God—Grace tells of what Christ has done for man.

The law bears on a nature prone to disobedience—Grace creates a nature inclined to obedience.

The law addresses man as part of the old creation—Grace makes man a member of the new creation.

The law demands obedience by the terrors of the law—Grace beseeches men by the mercies of God.

The law demands holiness—Grace gives holiness.

The law says: Condemn him—Grace says: Embrace him.

These truths cause us to know that without the intervention of saving grace, all the gates of mercy would have been forever closed. The Word declares, "That as sin has reigned with death, even so might grace reign through righteousness unto everlasting life of Jesus Christ our Lord" (Rom. 5:21).

All of this makes us to sing with joy and gratitude in our hearts, the words of Charles Wesley;

> "Grace to cover all my sin;
>   Let the healing streams abound;
> Make and keep me pure within:
>   Thou of life the fountain art,
> Freely let me take of Thee;
>   Spring Thou up within my heart,
> Rise to all eternity."

About the Author

DR. ROBERT GREENE LEE is considered one of the greatest preachers in Christendom. He is pastor emeritus of the Bellevue Baptist Church, Memphis, Tennessee. He pastored at that historic church from 1927 to 1960.

Dr. Lee served three consecutive terms as president of the Southern Baptist Convention and four times as president of the Tennessee Baptist Convention. Dr. Lee has preached between 8,000 and 9,000 sermons, published over fifty books, and traveled millions of miles preaching the Word.

He is a graduate of Furman University and the Chicago Law School. He is a recipient of fourteen honorary degrees. He is enshrined in the "Christian Hall of Fame" at the Canton Baptist Temple, Canton, Ohio.

Among his earlier pastorates were First Baptist Church of New Orleans, Louisiana, and Citadel Square of Charleston, South Carolina.

Other current Broadman books by R. G. Lee are *Payday Everyday* and *Grapes from Gospel Vines*.

Other Broadman Books by R. G. Lee

GRAPES FROM GOSPEL VINES

Dr. Lee presents his Grapes with the hope that they "will help all readers to find comfort in sorrow—and to face perilous situations with wiser minds and stronger faith."

These messages are chock-full of "Leeism's."

PAYDAY EVERYDAY

Payday Everyday is the memoirs of a preacher often referred to as one of the greatest in the history of Christendom. Written in his own words, here is pure, unvarnished Lee, which means a delight for young and old. This book sparkles with humor, poignancy, exaltation of Christ, and the glory of the Christian calling.

Dr. Lee shares the experiences of his pastorates—many rib-tickling and many heartbreaking glances into his boyhood, his education, his visit to New Orleans as a laborer; an entire chapter devoted to humorous stories, sections of Dr. Lee's preaching, and more!